P9-DGE-899

TIM GABRIELSON

Tim Gabrielson's

Lemons to Laughter

Design and page layout by Paul Tietjen

Edited by Diana Rankin and John Tschida

ISBN 978-0-615-26334-2

For questions and reduced rate bulk orders please contact:

tim@keepitfunny.com

For more information on Tim please visit:

www.keepitfunny.com

"Make someone laugh today; even if it's only you!"
– Tim Gabrielson

Acknowledgements

I think this is the most difficult section of the book. No one is more aware than I of how little I actually know, and that producing this book is very much a team effort. So, as always, I'll do my best to mention some of the key players and realize that there will be many people not mentioned that should be. To those inadvertently left out, please forgive me. Know that you are in my heart.

To my wife and best friend, Rebecca: Thank you for being my biggest fan and for allowing me so much time on the road and in front of my computer. Thanks for your continued support and help with this and all my projects. Having a full-time job of your own and still always finding time to help me is just one of the many reasons I know I am blessed. I am lucky to have you in my life.

To my Mom and Dad, Dave and Arlene: Thank you for always being there and supporting me on whatever path I take. Thank you for being 'real' and giving me roots on which to stand. I love you more than life itself, and treasure the fact that God chose me to be your son.

To my dear friend, Diana Rankin: Thank you for spending the last five years writing and rewriting all my letters, promotional material, web information and of course, editing this book. I can't thank you enough for seeing this project through and spending countless hours of reading, editing, and pushing me to keep writing. Without you and your friendship this book would truly not have happened.

To my brother-in-law John Tschida: You are one of the most talented writers/speakers I know. Thank you for being a driving force behind putting more of me in this book. Thank you for your many hours of editing, meetings, emails, and phone calls to make this book better.

To my friend and lawyer, Justin Johnson: Thank you for all the advice, encouragement and support. Oh, and of course, for all the guys' nights out.

To my manager, Josh, and his wife, Tia Wainright: Thank you for your friendship, inspiration and support in guiding me into keynote speaking and worldwide corporate entertainment. Rebecca and I are very grateful to be part of the family. Without your vision, this book may still be on the back burner.

To my friend, Nick Anthony: Thanks for being a great sounding board and for pushing me to be the best I can be. (You should join the Army.) For always being honest, even if it hurts; thank you.

To the makers of the Keurig coffee brewer, the team at Vision Van Gough, and the rest of my family, friends, and fans: Thank you for all your emails, calls, and support during my life and my career. Truly, it is all of you that keep me doing what I love.

Ideas in this book were compiled from the obscure nooks and crannies throughout the grey matter that comprise my brain as well as help from the Internet, magazines, books, TV, and friends. If an idea in this book is similar to one you've thought of and you feel the credit has not been given to you, I'm giving it to you now.

Thanks for making me laugh!

Disclaimer

I regret we live in a society in which I have to issue a disclaimer for a book on how to live a healthier and happier life. However for those lacking the ability to reason, I say this:

The suggestions from this book on how to keep life funny are purely for entertainment. I do not endorse performing any of these practical jokes and vehemently advise against any actions that will cause harm to person or property. It is one thing to dream or fantasize about the pranks, but quite another to actually perform them. Dreaming is not a crime, but taking action may be!

Tim Gabrielson, dba Magic Man, Inc. is not responsible for any damage to person or property or any actions, reactions or repercussions resulting from acting out the gags within this book, described on the KeepItFunny.com website, or any of Tim's live performances.

TIM GABRIELSON

Preface

Early in 1986, at the ripe old age of 13, my family (trailer in tow) packed ourselves into a black Ford Escort and headed out on our first two-week road trip from Braham, Minnesota, all the way to the west coast. At 13, the Escort seemed to offer all the room I needed to endure my brother's torments. One of our stops was in Orange County, CA; at ,you guessed it, Disneyland. Memories of a huge shark named Jaws coming out of the water and nearly eating my entire family and the tears from being lost in the caves, thinking I would never see my parents again, are distant. But the man behind the counter of Merlin's Magic Shop (which closed later that year) will always be a part of my life. My wide-eyed curiosity at all of the wonders I was investigating in the shop were suddenly stopped when a man from behind a counter asked, "Do you want to see some magic?" I quickly fixed my gaze to him as he proceeded to make a red ball vanish from one hand ending up in the other. Somehow the balls then vanished and ended up in my hand. From that moment I was hooked.

I convinced my parents that I needed this trick, and the man behind the counter gladly sold it to us and even up-sold the parents by selling me (them) a book called *Now You See It. Now You Don't*, by Bill Tarr. This book is still one of the best of its kind for those who want to learn the fundamentals of magic. The rest of our trip and the entire ride home became a mission to learn the red ball trick. By the time we landed back in our Midwestern driveway, I had mastered that original move to make a ball vanish. I still do it in my act today.

I was entranced by all things magic. At this moment on my bookshelf before me sits a picture of a teacher, Oscar Peterson, from my home town. He was not only a family friend, he was a magician. Before Oscar passed away, I remember watching him perform, while thinking how much I wanted to be a magician.

Over the next few years, I acquired the secrets of one trick after another and would occasionally demonstrate my prowess by putting on shows for the family. I was even getting hired to do a few birthday parties. It wasn't until I worked at a theme park –as an actor– that I began to realize magic could become a way of life. I was 16.

It was at Mission Creek Park, I befriended the staff magician, Franko. He showed me my first card trick and it blew me away. That feeling of awe and wonder is indescribable. It's so amazing what you can do to the mind with a simple magic trick. Franko helped me to improve things I already knew while adding lots more to my growing arsenal. I worked my way up to about 30 minutes of material, and then it happened. Franko told me to do the show in his place. "It's just improv," he said. "Go wing it." Easy for him to say! I hit the stage in a cold sweat, stared out over the top of my huge audience, and raced through my material in about ten minutes. Was the show good? Probably not. But I loved it. This is where it began. Throughout my years working at Mission Creek, I had the pleasure of watching several magicians. One of them was Michael Madden. He was (aside from

Franko) the first magician I saw who completely owned the crowd. His timing was amazing. His ability to engage the crowd was like nothing I'd ever seen before. The passion to be that guy on stage grew in me. It became my focus, my goal. I worked hard. I studied all the magicians who came through to perform. Each was a learning opportunity for me to fine-tune my skills.

Before long, I reached my goal. I became 'the' magician at the park. As Hamburg, Germany, was to the Beatles, so Mission Creek was to me. I did three shows a day, six days a week. Every unpredictable situation that arose, be it comments from the crowd or hecklers, I was ready. It forced me to improvise, to respond quickly and creatively with words as well as facial expressions. I quickly learned it wasn't just about the tricks. It was about how I could make people feel before, during and after the tricks. My job was to entertain, not just do magic.

People responded to the humor. This is where the "keep it funny" philosophy was born and success followed. I was given the opportunity to open for artists such as Garth Brooks, Alan Jackson, and Johnny Cash. Over time, as my career continued to grow, so did the opportunities. I have been blessed with the chance to perform in more than thirty states before Fortune 500 companies, fairs, colleges and a number of televised performances, including four times on the "Crook & Chase" show, The "Jerry Lewis Telethon", and E! Entertainment's "Talk Soup" I now not only fill in for Vegas headliners, but landed a six-month stint as a Vegas headliner, with my own show called "The Magic of Comedy." Who knew that a simple vanishing ball would take me from the poorly lit halls of Merlin's Magic Shop to the neon lights of the Vegas strip? I am literally living a dream.

As I look back at my journey, I wish that was the whole story. It wasn't always a smooth ride. There were (and continue to be) many ups and downs. At times I still feel like I'm in the back of that bumpy Escort making its way back home. Some of those bumps I created myself.

Thinking back about 18 years, I remember being very confident in what I was doing. People loved my show, almost as much as I loved doing it. I think my insecurity as a young performer made me appear cocky at times. I certainly didn't realize it then, but some people sure did. I will never forget one particular show, at an outdoor fair, where I pulled a guy out of the audience to participate onstage. As I often did then, I continued to poke fun at him, getting the same laughs I was accustomed to receiving. But then something happened that had never happened before. I saw – much too late –the gentleman was taking my patter very seriously, to the point that his embarrassment turned into a small tear. I quickly tried to 'joke' it off, which was the worst approach I could have taken. He stopped my show by getting so angry that he walked offstage. The crowd quickly turned on me and I was never hired by that fair again.

This incident hit me hard. What am I doing? I asked myself. My guilt had me wondering if I shouldn't get a "real job"; I felt so bad. But, there was the next show to do, and the next after that. I soon realized it's not the mistakes we make, but what we learn from them that matter. To this day I still feel bad about what happened, but as I look back, this was a fundamental turning point in my life. That experience made me realize that the show is not about me. It's about making people feel better about themselves, giving people hope, and giving them a break from the lemons this world often gives them. Not to throw more lemons at them. Now, don't get me wrong, I still poke fun, but it comes from a much different place. I will push someone's limits onstage, but I do everything to make sure they are having fun, too. We laugh together, we enjoy the experience and my goal now is to help people learn to laugh at themselves. Without that tough day at the fair, I don't think I would be writing this today.

The five-year journey of writing this book, and my passion for keynote speeches (on topics such as how laughter serves a higher purpose for any organization and how to have a fun work environment) all started in Reno, Nevada. There, I was working in the *Sammy Davis Jr. Room* at Harrah's Casino and finishing my 31st show in a seven-week run. It was hot. I was tired and in a rotten mood. I wanted nothing more than to go back to my dressing room and relax. The last thing I wanted to do that day was go through the "meet-and-greet" after the show. But, I knew it was the right thing to do. I plastered on a fake smile and politely answered questions and acknowledged compliments from audience members, all the while wondering when these silly exchanges would end. After what seemed like an eternity, I heaved a sigh of relief and prepared to leave. As I walked towards the stage, I saw a woman sitting at a table close by waving me over. No less tired, but curious; I approached her. She was crying quietly and had been for some time, it appeared. Her tremulous smile broke my heart as she told me her story.

"...I lost my husband six months ago," she said. "I haven't been able to get my mind off of the loss and haven't really found anything to smile about, either. I was told that I should come out for the day to see a show. Young man, for an hour I did not think about my loss. I didn't think about any of my troubles. All I did was laugh. I laughed so hard I cried. Your show gave me an hour to forget everything, but how to laugh..."

I was reminded at that moment that laughter is a gift. It's a gift we give ourselves and we allow others to give back to us. That experience reminded me that every day I wake up; I make the CHOICE to have a good day. It's a choice we all make. That lovely lady reminded me of why I'm here.

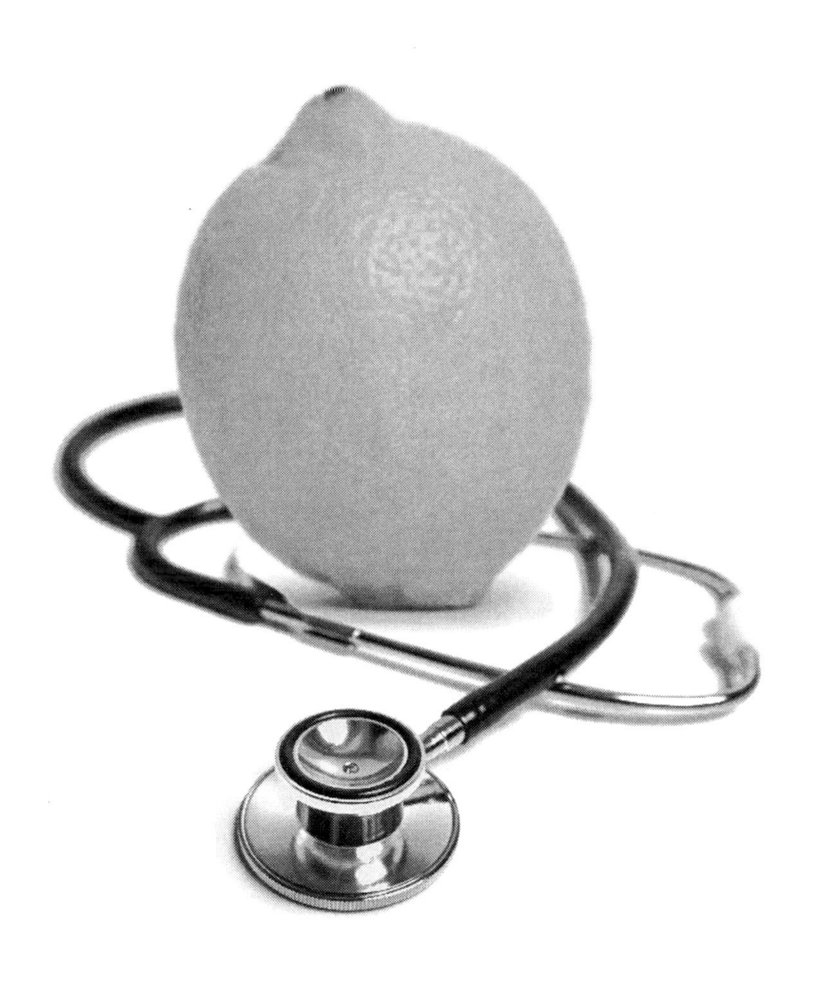

Chapter 1

Benefits of Laughter

One of my favorite things about being a performer is watching the laughter and joy in my audience. I have the privilege of standing in front of them doing the over-the-top things most wish they had the nerve or opportunity to do; which in turn ensures we all have a good time. That's an amazing gig! It's even more fun when I bring someone from the audience into the show and let them enjoy that moment of freedom with me.

How many people would put on a dorky hat or go along with a joke they're obviously going to be the butt of *just because*? Not many. But, when they step up on stage, they're suddenly willing to do things that would never have occurred to them before. That's the magic of performance. But, there's more to it than that. People, as a rule, want to laugh. Most people are willing to make a fool of themselves if it means getting a laugh, but they don't know how or where to begin. When I pull them up on stage with me, it gives them permission to let loose and go along with the fun.

The truth is that if everyone felt a little more comfortable doing that kind of thing out of the spotlight (and as part of everyday life), the world would be a lot more fun. Who wouldn't love watching someone swimming in a public fountain in the middle of New York City? How much fun would it be to break into song in a store and have others follow suit? Now that's good stuff! Enjoying yourself shouldn't need to be scripted or part of a performance; it should seep into every experience you have from work and school to hanging out with friends at home. The way to do that is to refuse to take yourself too seriously. Instead, play along whenever the opportunity arises. Better yet, be your own performer and guide your audience toward a great time.

This book is meant to help you find your own muse. It's a guide of sorts to help you learn the tricks and tempo of keeping it funny. Life is going to throw you lemons, that's a given. However, after reading this book I hope you will have an arsenal of opportunities to turn those lemons into laughter. It will be a challenge for some, while for others it will be second nature. For those who question the importance of finding laughter in your life, just look to your mental and physical well-being to realize its importance.

A. It's All in Your Mind

Humor works as the ultimate cure for the emotional strain endured through everyday life. Sure, some need a prescription to address serious mental health issues, but why is it that we as a society jump so quickly to things like Prozac® when laughter, change of diet and exercise may be all you need? Not that long ago, drugs of its kind didn't even exist. As generations have done before us, use your wit to relieve anger, frustration and sadness. I hope most will agree it is the tried and true method of survival. Lifting one's spirits in the midst of tragedy offers a chance at hope for better times, and makes getting through the trauma much easier for all involved.

It's remarkable what stress and depression can do to the mind. Aside from the headaches and muscle tension, there is an alarming list of problems that result from the pressure of everyday life when you allow it to overtake you:

Insomnia
Lack of concentration
Irritability
Memory loss
Isolation
Overreactions

The human mind has a tendency to distort reality to its limits; often to the negative extreme. With this shift in perspective comes a shift in stress on the body. The bigger a problem seems, the harder it is to solve; which creates even more stress perpetuating a circular crisis. Psychologists have long believed that people who laugh during troubling times have a better perspective on problems; reducing them to tolerable (and more realistic) levels.

As you laugh at the problems facing you, they have less power over you and seem more manageable. In the end, the perception is what guides it and laughter changes perception in a positive way. It's not always easy to find the humor in a given situation. It takes practice, but it can be done. And while a specific situation may not seem humorous, surrounding situations just might.

Finding the humor during a difficult time forces you to think outside the box; expanding your mind and removing yourself from the close confines of the problem. Remaining in the crisis is the easy answer, but to find something funny means you're expanding your foundation and by default; your mind. Narrow, focused thinking of any sort can bring on stress, and when that focus is on trauma... well, you see where this is going. Laughter pulls you out of the situation and plops you down in a better place to assess the true damage and make plans for how to resolve it.

A recent study by Prof. Bruce Charlton out of the University of Newcastle in the UK indicates we're all starting to be a little more flexible and childlike. His theory, called psychological neoteny, claims that people are taking longer to mature, if they ever do. This comes from the increased changes and mobility in our society. Add to that the prolonged time adults are going to school, where the mind is required to be more receptive to new learning and cognitive flexibility, and the rigid mentality of 50 or 100 years ago seems to be fading away.

"When formal education continues into the early twenties," Charlton says, "it probably, to an extent, counteracts the attainment of psychological maturity, which would otherwise occur at about this age." The end result is a society of highly successful adults who prefer to think outside the box, and don't get stuck in a formal, unyielding process of development.

Even the experts are saying that immaturity has its benefits! It relieves stress and leads to highly successful people. And we've not even gotten to the most important part. If you want to jump start it, you might want to check out the "Brain Age" game; it is intended to decrease the brain age of aging adults.

B. It's a Physical Thing

There have been many studies conducted through the years showing the physical benefits of laughter. From claims of increased blood flow to an actual boost in life expectancy, doctors and researchers continue to exhort the correlation between laughter and good health.

None of this is news to those with a healthy sense of humor. They've experienced first-hand the health benefits of laughter, and rarely have the problems that come from a more sedate lifestyle. Sometimes, however, it requires seeing it in print for it to ring true.

In 2005, the University Of Maryland School Of Medicine published a study of the physical payback of humor on the cardiovascular system. By showing 20 participants 15 minutes each of two separate movies – one to induce stress, the other to induce humor – researchers found that humor acts as a vasodilator. This means that the blood vessels react to humor in such a way as to dilate, or open, to allow better blood flow due to the expansion of the endothelium, or inner lining of the blood vessels. On the flip side, the stressful movie acted as a vasoconstrictor, meaning it tightened the blood vessels, lowering the blood flow.

While 20 participants isn't a particularly large segment for a study, the interesting outcome was the percentage of people positively affected by humor. In the stress portion of the study, 70 percent had a vasoconstriction reaction. In the humor portion of the study, however, 95 percent had a positive effect of increased blood flow. Rescarchers concluded that humor has a direct and positive effect on the body. Who would have guessed it?

Consider my family history. My grandfather suffered a heart attack at the age of 25, followed by three open heart surgeries in his remaining 59 years of life. My father underwent angioplasty at the ripe young age of 50. It should come as no surprise that research on the effect of laughter upon the heart would make its way into this book. Watching the most important man in my life and his father undergo these procedures gave me a strong desire to protect myself from a similar fate using any and all available tactics I could get my hands on. Discovering that laughter is one of the better preventative medicines was a blessing to me. That's a lot more fun than a bland diet and exercise!

According to the University of Maryland School of Medicine's Dr. Michael Miller, M.D., the principal investigator and director of preventative cardiology, "The endothelium is the first line in the development of atherosclerosis or hardening of the arteries, so, given the results of our study, it is conceivable that laughing may be important to maintain a healthy endothelium, and reduce the risk of cardiovascular disease. At the very least, laughter offsets the impact of mental stress, which is harmful to the endothelium."

As I understand, this means that laughter can prevent a broken heart. It does a lot of other things as well. Laughter is credited with:

Reducing stress
Lowering blood pressure
Boosting the immune system
Improving brain function
Protecting the heart
Burning calories and building muscles

Physically, laughter can make your most vital organs stronger, your body more toned and your face shine. But who needs studies to prove that laughter makes you feel better? Do you remember the last good, tear-jerking laugh you had? How it made your sides ache, your lungs gasp for breath and your head clear? Heck, if it was a *really* good one, you were likely sweating when all was said and done. Laughing is a work out, both inside and out, and not the kind you need tights and a medicine ball for, either. A couple of good friends, a table, great stories, and ta-da! The calories just melt away, along with the stress of everyday life. When stress fades, so do the chemicals in the body that can damage cells. Cortisols, created by the adrenal cortex in response to stress, have a positive purpose in short bursts, but the long-term effects are frightening. Aside from the additional physical stress on the body, extreme levels of cortisols can be attributed to heart disease, high blood pressure, and stroke, as well as a host of other illnesses. The tension-release mechanism that occurs in laughter results in relaxed muscles, which helps guide the body toward a more relaxed state in general.

Turning a stressful moment into a laughter-filled one promotes a healthy outlook. It eliminates the importance put on the little stuff, and allows us to remember not to take life quite so seriously.

C. Live, Love, Laugh

In my opinion, a good sense of humor is tied to self-respect and the ability to laugh at oneself. This shows a healthy self esteem as well as an acceptance of who you are. The lack of a sense of humor, therefore, is tied directly to poor self-esteem. It should be no surprise that in addition to good health and mental well-being, humor lends itself to a certain level of popularity. Laughter builds unity and companionship, so it should be no surprise that people flock to those with a strong sense of self as well as those who make them laugh. Sharing a laugh releases the tension of new relationships; giving people something simple, easy and fun to enjoy together. It's impossible, after all, to feel anxiety and truly laugh at the same time. In fact, it's impossible to feel angry, depressed, guilty or jealous while having a good belly laugh, too. Try it sometime.

What it all comes down to is an appreciation for the absurdity of life. All things being equal, there just isn't much that can be done to alleviate the minor traumas and daily difficulties everyone endures. So rather than try; find humor in them. One can't take things too seriously without it affecting every aspect of life; the same can be said for taking life lightly. Humor enjoins, attracts, relieves and grows. It's the glue in relationships and the strength in families.

After a round of golf at a beautiful course in Arizona, my wife and I accompanied our friends, Glen and Kate, to the home of one of their friends. Having never met these folks before, my wife, Rebecca, and I were chatting about how tense these "meeting new people" situations can be. You can imagine our surprise when the host answered the door wearing only a wrestling leotard! What a great ice breaker and tension reliever! I'm certainly not advising anyone to do this; however, the tone was set from the moment we arrived and laughter continued throughout the night.

The joy of friendship (be it new friends or old) comes with the added bonus of forgiveness. Use this to your advantage. Friends can become the best "victims" of your pranks.

- Before your friends arrive to your home for the party, pour a liberal amount of detergent into the toilet tank. Imagine the fun you will have as the next guest flushes the toilet resulting in lots of bubbles.

- In our house we have a small half bath off the kitchen, so when we have friends over and someone dares to use it, they know they risk lack of privacy. I like to put a bunch of bubble wrap underneath the seat, so when they exit after sitting and popping a bunch of bubbles, they will feel the need to explain.
- One day prior to a gathering at your home, fill some wine glasses with Jell-O (cranberry for the red and lemon for the white). Have them set and ready in the fridge. After the first glass or two of real wine, substitute the Jell-O for the next glass and watch the faces as the confusion occurs; very funny! Worth the set up.
- Fill your medicine cabinet with marbles before a party.
- Buy a cheap travel alarm; set the alarm for morning commute time and hide it in your friend's car. Better yet; set a bunch to go off in three minute intervals and hide them all over in your friend's house or apartment.
- Fill your umbrellas with confetti; in case of rain, always offer yours.
- Reset all of your friend's radio stations in the car.
- Re-program all of the speed-dial phone numbers on a friend's phone to your number.
- Insist on calling your friends by entirely different names, like Biff, Taffy or my favorite, Scooter.
- Add green food coloring to someone's milk.

- Put an Alka-Seltzer™ tablet in the showerhead.
- Tape a $5 bill to the end of your fishing line, then cast the line out while you hide behind a bush; reel it in slowly when someone bends over to pick it up.
- Hang the end of a spool of thread out of your shirt pocket and when someone goes to take it off for you watch their face as more and more string comes out in their hand.
- Put your face really close to theirs while they're facing a different direction, tap them on the shoulder, and watch them jump when they turn to face you.
- Pretend you don't understand what they're saying, no matter how much they yell and how slowly they say it.
- Put a "For Sale by neighbor" Sign in your neighbor's front yard; leave his number, if you have it.
- For the golfers out there, next time you are in a scramble or best ball tournament, take along a bag of marshmallows and throw them in the cooler. Randomly drop a few during the day and watch as your friends in the group behind keep mistaking them for golf balls. They will fall for it over and over again.
- Get about three other people in on a joke that has no meaning at all, and tell it with those three people and the "victim" in the room. All the people 'in' on the joke laugh, and the victim doesn't get it. However, it's best when they pretend they do. My favorite is, "a hippo and a penguin are taking a bath. The hippo

says, 'pass the soap.' And the penguin says 'no soap' Radio!" This is a classic.

- Before the order arrives at a restaurant with a candle on the middle of the table, in your "victim's" absence, take one of their plates, hold the bottom rim over the candle, and rotate it so you get a lot of soot on the bottom of the plate, When they come back, say, " I'm going to hypnotize you. Pick up your plate in your left hand, and with your right hand, copy all my actions." Proceed to rub your index finger around the bottom rim of your plate, and in a circle on your forehead, then around the rim, and each of your eyes. Keep going, with different parts of the face, until they notice.

- Every time you go out to eat with friends, as the waiter comes over to take your table's order, quickly say, "why don't we let the birthday boy/girl go first?" If your friend doesn't think fast enough and just smiles and gives their order, they will most likely have to deal with the embarrassing birthday candles and song.

- Disguise your voice and leave the following message on a friend's answering machine: 'Sir, we're not sure if you wanted us to do it, you know, after what happened, so, well, we went ahead and did it anyway. If you don't like it, we can probably take it out, but we'll have to charge you extra. Please return this call immediately, Thanks."

Be sure that your pranks are fun in nature; rather than hurtful, and they'll be laughing right alongside you. It may even spur a little competition that keeps the humor going for months. Everyday could bring a new surprise.

Pranks are just one of the ways to engage people and have a good laugh. For some of you, the thought of fighting a grizzly bear with one arm tied behind your back may be more enticing than actually releasing the fears and inhibitions prohibiting you from acting these out. Do not feel frustrated. It's like school was for me at times, and not just because of the trouble I had in middle school (that I will share a bit of in the next chapter). I watched my friends enjoying full social lives (which seemed to include NO studying or homework time) and pulling A's and B's, while I worked like a fiend to get the same results. The point is, some of you will have to work harder than others, but in the end it will be worth it. I promise. Start slow, try the easy ones first and work your way up. How, you ask? Well, whenever I was nervous about starting conversations or uncomfortable in unfamiliar surroundings (yes, I was a bit reserved), magic tricks became the perfect opportunity to both engage and surprise people.

I can still remember the feeling of accomplishment I had at the age of 13 when I was finally able to fool my Mom with the first magic trick I learned; the 'red ball' trick. The look of amazement was genuine and it gave me an unexplainable but immediate boost of confidence. The reward was two-fold. My insecurities seemed to vanish the more I performed the trick (for increasing numbers of people) and it always made them feel better, too. For the next few years, I never left home without a trick on hand.

Magic can be an ice-breaker for those of you who may be a bit more reserved (or even insecure). As I mentioned before, it will lighten the mood and allow people to open up to the idea of "keeping it funny". I have been a full time entertainer for over 15 years and I can confidently say that magic has not only become my business, it has been a great tool for meeting friends, boosting sales at various jobs and helping me through some really tough junior-high years. Best of all; it's how I met my wife.

There are literally thousands of magic tricks you can learn. Where do you start? Well, if you are interested in some magic that I think is really cool, you can check out my DVD and some other easy-to-learn magic effects at www.keepitfunnystore.com. With a little practice, you'll be the life of the party in no time.
Cards are probably the easiest (and least expensive) props to find. I'll teach you a few fundamental card secrets (and how you can turn those fundamentals into some really cool tricks) to get you on your way. Here are a few from the 52 (sorry for the rhyme) card ticks in my magic kit called "A full deck of card tricks".

The Key Card

Have a spectator shuffle a deck of cards. When you get it back, secretly look at the bottom card. In our example we will say it is the Ace of Hearts. This card is your "key" card. Have the spectator cut the deck into four piles. Ask him to pick one of the piles. Look at the top card from that pile and replace the card. Take the pile containing the "key card" and place it on top of the pile with the selected card. This places the key card on top of the selected card. Place the rest of the piles on top of this one. The deck may be cut several times without fear of separation these two cards. Now, run through the deck until you see the key card (Ace of Hearts), the card next to it is the selected card.

Another way to find a card is to know what it is before the spectator even selects the card. To accomplish this you will need to know how to force a card (make the spectator pick the card you want). Here are two different ways to do this:

The Cross Cut Force

You have to be a bit bold to try this. Start with the card you want to be forced on the bottom of the deck. Have the spectator cut the deck in half separating both halves on the table. Place the bottom half of the deck on top in the form of a cross. Create misdirection for a few moments by talking about the trick, pick up the top portion of the cross, showing the bottom card, asking the spectator to look at the card he cut to. By creating the earlier misdirection, your spectator will not realize the 'cut to card' is really the original bottom card (force card). He will think it was the free selection.

10-20 Force

Place the card to be forced ninth from the top of the deck. Ask the spectator to name any number between 10 and 20. Add the two digits of the named number - subtract the chosen number and count down to the card in that position, Example: If the chosen number is 15, 1 plus 5 equals 6, 15 minus 6 equals 9. The result will always be 9.

Now with the ability to know the card ahead of time, imagine all the things you could do. This should get you started.

Sealed Prediction

Write the prediction, "You will pick the Ten of Spades" on a piece of paper and seal it in an envelope. Hand the envelope to a spectator to hold. Force the ten of Spades using one of the previous mentioned methods. Ask the spectator to open the envelope, revealing your future prediction.

The final trick is a version of the trick I used to meet a young lady I now call my wife over ten years prior to our wedding in 2004. I had her sign her name on a card before shuffling it in with the deck. I then had her spell out using the cards, one card placed on the table per letter *I will marry you someday* and on the last card she turned over her signed card. The someday was definitely longer than I planned; however the prediction proved to be much more than a card trick.

The Spelling Trick

Arrange six cards in the following order face-up on the table: Six of Clubs-Ten of Hearts-King of Spades-Eight of Hearts-Jack of Diamonds-Eight of Diamonds. Have a person think of one of these cards. Gather the cards and place them on the top of the deck. Secretly add nine cards to the top of the deck above the six cards. Ask the person to name the card he/she is thinking of. If it was the King of Spades, spell out King of Spades and as you spell the last letter turn over that card and show that it is his/her imagined card. This will work for any of the six cards.

Today
TUESDAY
January

Chapter 2

Every Day Fun

Life is full of opportunities to laugh, but you have to be willing to jump on them – sometimes literally. Rides in elevators, trips to the supermarket – these everyday aspects of life are chances for bend-over, hurt-your-gut laughter. It requires, however, the ability to let go of your inhibitions.

Your inhibitions are the little noises your brain makes, that sound remarkably like that relative, teacher or childhood neighbor who has implanted themselves in your conscience. This short-sighted voice is constantly reminding you to be at your best behavior. For the purpose of this book we'll call him Kill-joy. Our friend, Kill-joy, has a sour disposition and takes himself far too seriously. There are rules for everything in his life and an appropriate way to live. Structure and convention are his friends and any type of deviance is strictly not tolerated. The sorry soul.

If anyone needs a little loosening up, it's Kill-joy. After all, life on earth has the same end result for everyone. What sets us apart is how we get there and whether we laugh along the way. I'm sure you've heard that life is really about the journey. Well here's your chance to start enjoying every facet of your life while living a longer, happier existence in the process; all the while ignoring Kill-joy.

The problem with Kill-joy is that he's been with you a long time. Every time you consider making a fool of yourself for a giggle, he raises his ugly head, points that disapproving finger and makes you second-guess yourself. Learning to ignore him will be your greatest challenge in accepting a life of laughter. I'm not saying that Kill-joy didn't laugh. I'm sure you've both had a few good laughs in your lifetime. But, have either of you been the butt of a joke that to this day makes you bend over laughing so hard you're hoping the seams in your pants hold? Or do you instead hide in a corner until the blush diminishes and the funny feeling of shame fades away?

A. You, too, can be silly

Being silly is a state of mind. It's learning to laugh at yourself before anyone else can, and it involves some serious tutorials... or some not so serious tutorials… or something like that. Basically, it is learning to ignore Kill-joy and trip along to your own whims, ignoring convention and protocol.

Start out by recognizing your own insecurities. What sets you off? What are you most afraid of someone knowing about and using against you? What is it that makes you cringe just to think about it? We all have those memories hidden away somewhere. Some are more deeply buried than others.

For me, one of those events took place during a middle school gym class kickball game. I'll probably never understand the reasoning behind social "cliques" and their ability to divide the cool and not-so-cool, with one group often inflicting pain on the other. That day in the gymnasium I was on the receiving end, and it certainly imprinted my soul and laid the groundwork for a good dose of insecurities for years to come.

As I awaited my turn at the plate, I heard a chant from my classmates start faintly at first, but it grew louder and more distinct with each repetition. "PAT, PAT, PAT, PAT....". My heart sank and embarrassment washed over me, as I realized the entire team was focused on me and the acronym they had so ungraciously assigned: People Against Tim. This was only a glimpse of the childish display of bullying I experienced but this one still lingers in the back of my head from time to time.

Situations like this become our trigger points, our fears and reservations. These are the things that can hold us back and prevent us from finding humor in all things if we let them. It is unfortunate that people can be so cruel. But remember; we can't control the actions of others; we can, however, control our reactions. It would be easy to turn situations like the one in that gym class into a seed of despair that continues to grow over time, eventually overtaking every ounce of self-esteem and happiness. However, using these trigger-points as learning experiences not only makes us stronger, but provides us with empathy. It is much more difficult, but far more rewarding to move beyond these experiences. This middle school trial, as painful as it was, helped prepare me for difficult and challenging experiences. It also instilled in me the desire to help others find joy despite their own insecurities.

Where do we go from here? Well, it's just a matter of letting go of the kickball games in the distant past and the fear of shame that comes from being the butt of a prank or joke. If you accept who you are, the whole and complete picture, you can learn to laugh at the things that used to make you cringe. After all, every part of your personality makes you special and unique and there's nothing more attractive than someone who recognizes that and finds joy in it.

Have you ever seen someone singing and dancing to the overhead songs at the music store? Did it make you smile? How about the grown-up in the toy store who can't help but play with the pogo stick? I love to watch that kind of freedom unleash itself! That's someone who's comfortable with him or herself. That's someone I want to get to know. When you can do the same , that's what people will think about you. So let loose a little and see what happens.

I remember a particular show of mine at a fair in Nevada. Having just finished dinner with a few of the fair board members (the ones that had my check), we began making our way to the office with our empty plates still in hand. Without missing a beat, I handed my plate to a passerby while asking "...Can you hold onto this for a second?"... You should have seen the dumbfounded expression on his face as I continued walking with the group. Now I know that might sound a bit bold, but everyone (including the guy left holding my plate) got a lot of enjoyment out of it. The fair board members recalled it as that fair's highlight. When you try silly things like this, you'll be amazed at the changes, both in how others see you and in how you see yourself.

B. Start Slowly; Think Young

I won't lie to you. This is going to hurt a little; at least at first. There's a lot of social programming that suggests being silly is for children, and while that's true, it's been misinterpreted. Being silly is for children, yes, but it's not *only* for children. That's where we've gone completely haywire. We're letting the kids have all the fun!

Remember Professor Charlton and his study on immaturity? It's time to put that theory into practice and see just how far we can bring it home. This is for your own good, after all. Ignoring your more mature side will give you a lift in all you do and help you succeed. So, just how childlike can you be?

Watching a child playing by himself is a lot like watching a documentary on how to have fun. They couldn't care less what "The Rules" (and Kill-joy) say. They just do what makes them happy. The rigidity of cleanliness, insecurities and maturity that constrict and define adult behavior has no place in a child's mentality. It shouldn't always in an adult's, either. Where is it written that playing with mud is wrong once we get past the second grade? Since when has adulthood been synonymous with dull?

The challenge is being able to do these things without worrying too much about making a fool of yourself. Did I mention this was going to hurt? Letting go of those fears isn't always going to be easy. It's going to take a lot of faith, but it's worth it. And it sure beats feeling like a complete fool in front of the world. If you doubt the benefits, go back and re-read the first chapter. I mean, seriously, if all those doctors say it's a good thing, who are we to argue? Isn't it better to be an old fool in good health then a middle-aged frump with a bad ticker? You don't have to take my word for it. Check out the works of celebrated authors such as Norman Vincent Peale. He is just one of many that have spent a lifetime writing on similar philosophies.

At the end of the day, this is a control thing, and what may not have occurred to you is that by following the Rules of Conduct, you're allowing society to control what you do and ultimately who you are. Show some backbone! Eat a bug, for goodness sake, and thumb your nose at the silliness of the State of Maturity!

To get you started, here are some ways to have fun despite yourself:

- Walk into a store with a sign that says, "Have a penny? Give a penny! Need a penny? Take a penny!" with a HUGE jar of pennies. Take a penny out of the cup, put it into your jar, and walk out.
- When a couple of people are walking ahead of you, run between them yelling "Red Rover!"

- Make mud pies.
- Lay on the ground and spin in circles on your right side; do the same on your left.
- Roll down a hill.
- Catch fireflies and make rings and necklaces out of their lights; pretend to be rich and famous while you sashay around the yard in your new jewels.
- Make a snowman; have a snowball fight with him; let him win.
- Follow an ant to see where he goes.
- Skip.
- Pour a box of cornstarch into a shallow bucket and fill the bucket with water; you'll be amazed as the cornstarch refuses to get wet no matter what you do.
- Wear a pair of pants on your head.
- Eat your favorite kind of sweetened cereal for dinner.
- Sing "If I had a Hammer" very loudly in the grocery store.
- Make ten paper boats out of dollar bills and set them afloat in a public fountain.
- Read comic books in public.
- Everywhere you go, dart around suspiciously while humming the theme from "Mission: Impossible".
- Hold indoor shopping cart races.
- Make up nonsense products and ask newly hired employees if

there are any in stock.

- Randomly throw soft, light things over into neighboring aisles.
- Walk up to complete strangers and say, "Hi! I haven't seen you in so long!..." See if they play along to avoid embarrassment.
- Stick your palm open under the stall wall of the restroom and ask you neighbor "may I borrow a highlighter?"
- Try pants on backwards at the Gap. Tell the sales person that there is something wrong with these pants.
- At the bottom of an escalator, scream out "My Shoelaces!" AAAGH!
- Leave on the plastic string connecting a new pair of shoes and wander around the store.
- If you need to get through a big crowd; I like to yell out "excuse me, having a baby!" The crowd always parts.
  (Just helping you out.)

Having fun is the first step to laughing, which is the next step to living well; which is the ultimate goal, isn't it? Start by learning to enjoy the little things in life again, and maybe do something that will embarrass you a little so you remember how to laugh at yourself. From there, it's just a matter of baby steps to the next level.

C. Critics, Schmitics... "Who gives a hoot?"

Be prepared to defend yourself to the crazy people out there who honestly think that having fun at your own expense is wrong and shouldn't be tolerated. These are the people who get embarrassed when others act out and feel uncomfortable by your having fun. They glare at adults skipping through the store. They look down their noses at general horseplay. These are also the people who need your help the most. Like my Mom used to tell me, "You have to go with the flow and stay flexible or you will get bent out of shape."

When your antics find you faced with a nasty, wrinkled up prune face, you have two choices: ignore them and go about your business, or include them in your activities. On some level it seems almost cruel to ignore them. What sad little lives they must lead to feel such contempt for a bit of fun!

The critics will be there; that's a given. The rolled eyes, the crossed arms, the bunched up pantyhose and ugly floral dress will stare back at you from the crowd. Remember that these people aren't judging you for what you're doing, but rather for what they are uncomfortable doing. By inviting them into your games, you're helping them break through that shell of societal fear and giving them the tools to enjoy life just a little bit more. Plus, it's a heck of a lot of fun messing with the most judgmental of them.

In my show, I tend to look for the most hard-nosed audience member I can find. They stand out, so it's not difficult to spot them. Arms crossed, chin down, they are practically daring me to pick them. These are the people that I will do my best to try to make smile or maybe even pick on a bit. Why? I'm sure to some extent it is because I am insecure enough to think it is a personal attack on me; besides the fact that they are the ones who need it the most and usually end up having the most fun. I don't humiliate them. I just include them in the jokes and in no time at all, they've been able to relax and have the time of their lives. They just didn't know they wanted to play along. It's as if they needed permission to have fun; which I gladly granted.

I'll never forget a guy named Bill during a show for Ducks Unlimited in Sioux Falls, South Dakota. As the show began, I noticed him in the front rolling his eyes at those he was with, but he never looked directly at me. "Well that's not going to work for me," I told myself as I jumped off the stage, positioning myself directly in front of this shirt-and-tie clad burly grump. I addressed the entire crowd as I said "one of my favorite parts of the show is to walk out into the audience and stand next to someone. You see, when you stand next to someone they look away and do not make eye contact with you." I lowered my head and in a squeaky voice mimicked the picture I was painting for the crowd. "If I don't look, he won't pick me." Bill looked up at me, "Except for you, sir. You are looking directly at me. I think you will enjoy the show more if you give it a chance and watch it." As the show progressed, I continued to address cracks towards him and to my surprise, by the end of the show he was rolling with laughter. Later he came up to me and said, "As you could tell, the last place I wanted to be was watching a 'magician,' but you were so much more than that. You were a riot. Thanks for making me laugh. I really needed it." Even the tough ones need to laugh.

When someone gives you a similar "look of disgust", do this:

- Walk up to him, look him squarely in the eye and say, "Meep!" then scamper away.
- Start laughing; laugh harder; keep laughing until they laugh with you. (don't worry, they will)
- Dodge behind them and sneak a peek over their shoulder as if trying to see what they're looking at; feign shock when they turn to see what you're doing.
- Ask them to hold your coat while you do cartwheels around them; this is even funnier if you don't know how to do them.
- Act like you're going to tickle them, but don't actually touch them.
- Stand behind them and make farting noises with your hands.
- Drape a blanket around your shoulders and run around saying, "I'm Batman, Come, Robin—to the bat cave!"
- Stare them in the face, and say "chase me!" and then run away.
- Stare, grinning, at them for a while and then announce: "I've got new socks on!

Remember, the goal is to rid the world of a judgmental attitude, so don't go over the top and make these people feel too ridiculous. Some people honestly can't handle laughing at themselves, or they may not recognize how judgmental they've become. They are playing by "the rules", after all. When they won't – or can't – go along with the fun, it's time to ignore the distaste on their faces and move on. There just isn't enough time to bother with those who choose not to be converted to a life of laughter and fun.

D. Big Changes from Small Moments

Every moment of each day is a chance to laugh. It's just a matter of recognizing and seizing the opportunities. A walk around the park can become a series of cartwheels, a game of tag or a moment of intrigue through espionage, but only if you are willing to take the risk of looking ridiculous.

It's not like I am telling you to wear your pants down to your knees like some of the kids today. I spotted one of these 'saggers' outside of the JBK commons area prior to a show at West Texas A&M University. This college student held a Starbucks Frappuccino in one hand and his laptop in the other. I could see the wheels in his head spinning as he was wondering how to move without a free hand to hold up his pants. After a few moments, he decided on a bowlegged waddle. I was bursting with laughter as I wondered what his major might be!

The point isn't to abandon your identity, but rather to improve and/or release it. Use the small moments to find joy, and from there it's an easy transition to laughing at the silliness we call everyday life. For some, this will feel impossible. For others it will be, well, a walk (or a waddle) in the park. Find your comfort level and push the boundaries as often as you can until you can relax while doing the absurd.

This may take time. It won't all come at once for everyone and you shouldn't expect it will. But you can take small, incremental steps that will lead you in a positive and fun direction. Consider, for example, playing little games with yourself to help you get past the echoes of Kill-joy. The object is to find simple ways to be silly that amuse you, but don't bring too much attention. These are the baby steps you need to be able to ignore Kill-joy entirely as you move on to the bigger, more exotic – and fun - things.

I remember hearing a story about a guy that was painfully shy, and he hated it. We all know people who are comfortable in small groups with close knit friends and family, rather than in crowds or public places that leave us more open and vulnerable to unwanted attention. To break himself out of his shell, he decided to buy four dozen long-stemmed red roses and hand them out at a busy intersection to whatever ladies walked by. He was terrified at first, but by the time he'd given out his first dozen he was really starting to get into it. The women who received the roses would smile and often gave him a hug. He was amazed at the reactions he got and by the time the last rose was given away, not only had he had gotten past a pretty serious personal barrier, but he got a couple of phone numbers. Nice as that was; it wasn't his goal. He believed his shyness to be a problem in his life and he took steps to remedy it. There's a lesson here about the unintended and positive (though unexpected or planned) outcomes that can result from a low-risk activity. Now it's your turn. Take those baby steps. What do you have to lose?

Try whistling as you walk to your car at the end of the day. It doesn't matter if you sound like a nightingale or can't carry a tune; the point is to do something that goes against your grain a bit without bringing undo embarrassment. Once you feel comfortable with the whistling, move on to swinging your briefcase or handbag in an exaggerated way. Don't forget to whistle, too! As time moves on and these little things feel less embarrassing, you can add to your repertoire. Skip to the car or walk backwards. Little by little you'll crash through those overly serious boundaries that have been in place for too long, and you'll remember how to have fun and laugh more. It will change the way you approach life, one day at a time, in ways you may not see as possibilities today.

Eventually, wading in a public fountain during lunch hour will seem amateurish. You'll ignore the skeptics and learn to laugh at yourself. At the very least, you'll have learned not to take life quite so seriously and moved onto accepting and embracing that it's sometimes fun to do strange things just to see what might happen.

It takes a certain amount of courage to face the Kill-joys of the world.

It takes an even greater amount of courage to admit you might be one of them. In the end, the challenge is worth it. Whether it's confronting yourself or someone else, the overwhelming stress of always doing the right thing – because that's what's been drilled into us – can evaporate like a cloud of magician's smoke. Life becomes a series of great times with great people held together with laughter. And who knows? You may even recruit a few Kill-joys along the way!

Chapter 3

Home Is Where The Laughter Is…Or Should Be

Most people spend 60 percent of time in their homes wandering around in zombie-like states and patterns. Between chores, family pressure and constant outside harassment, coming home can be a nightmare of added stress to an already overfilled plate. Life is busy. Life is too busy and the pace of our routines has accelerated dramatically in recent years. Think about how you spent your evening at home last night. Was it fun? Could it have been? Take control of your home and let the laughter reign!

My wife has a difficult job that can sometimes overwhelm her. When she comes home at night, we do our best to keep things as light as possible because this is our spot for fun. Part of our responsibility to each other is to make that time as enjoyable as we can so that our time together is always great.

This should be your priority, too. Make your home a haven for humor. The day-to-day grind we call life can be enlivened with the smallest things making the biggest differences. Even the most complex tasks can be broken down into manageable bits with the addition of humor to the job.

A. Chores

We all know that life at home isn't easy. There are lists of chores that never seem to end and when you think you are getting closer to the end of that list, ten more things have been miraculously added. The lawn needs to be mowed, refrigerator is empty, the ants have found their way to the front sidewalk, the air conditioner is making a weird noise, the cat is sick, you're out of trash bags, and to top it off you have a crack in the windshield of your car. You get the idea. It's how we deal with life's lemons that we can control. You *have* to do chores, but you don't have to hate them. Rather than dreading the duties, come at them with a touch of pizzazz. Put on your favorite tunes as loud as you can stand and dig in; just remember to have fun. How do you have fun? Try these.

- Hide in a pile of leaves until someone walks by, then jump out and SCREAM!
- Try to rake the leaves out of the trees before they have a chance to fall; best done while your neighbors are outside.
- Pretend to be an English butler or a French maid while going about your chores; don't forget the snooty attitude and horrible accent.
- Mow the lawn in weird shapes rather than cleanly cut.
- While doing dishes, pretend a butter knife is a submarine trying to sink the plastic cups; have a spoon save it.
- Waltz with the shirts before folding them.
- Race with your spouse or children to see who can do the chore first; winner gets to pick the next activity.
- Clean the house, but put various items in the wrong places; see how long it takes someone to notice.

- Put a rubber band around the sprayer next to the faucet and aim it so the next person to use the sink will get soaked. Do you remember doing that as a kid?
- Write "they know why" or "because the voices told me to" in the note section of your checks while paying bills.

Chores don't have to be routine if you don't want them to be. Find a way to make each undertaking a unique experience, preferably one filled with laughter, and getting things done will be a treat rather than a… well, chore.

B. Laughing Alone

For some reason, laughing alone frightens many. Perhaps it conjures images of sitting in a padded room at a hospital for the insane, where you are unable to convince the doctors that you don't belong there. Maybe it's just a fear of being called insane. Who knows? The point is that laughing alone can be some of the best times you ever have. You can safely lose all inhibitions without worrying about it coming back at you since there's no one to point and call you names later.

This is your chance to hang loose and let go. Here's the time to look Kill-joy squarely in the eyes and say, "I don't have to listen to you," because you really don't. Take a few steps in this direction by disregarding all the rules that are "supposed" to regulate your life.

- Don't check your email all day.
- Go to a park and use the swing .
- Have dessert first.
- Go out to eat and pay with pennies.
- Wave at strangers.
- Decline to be seated at a restaurant and just eat a few of the mints at the host stand and walk out.
- Repeat everything someone says as a question.
- Go to a drive through and insist that your order is "to go!"
- When you talk to a stranger, occasionally bob your head like a parrot.
- Don't eat your peas. (Sorry Dad)
- Go out to eat by yourself and ask for a second seat for your "imaginary friend".
- Go to a place with a jukebox and play the same song over and over.
- Wear your pajamas all day; go for a long walk in them.
- Watch Saturday morning cartoons.
- Talk to the pets as if they were human; don't forget to pause for their answers to your questions.
- Practice your best dance moves.
- Create outlandish hairstyles with gel and mousse.

- Quote Richard III on your answering machine: "Now is the winter of our discontent made glorious summer by your name and number."
- Meow occasionally.
- Run around the house naked while playing Ray Stevens' "The Streak".

Ok, don't really run around naked, but sometimes when you're first learning to laugh at the ridiculous, this is how you feel: stripped completely down to the buff. It doesn't have to be like that. When something is funny, feel free to laugh at it. If you are asking yourself, "What is funny?" I say "funny is funny!" What ever makes you laugh is funny. There's no right or wrong and no definition to fit everyone reading this book. It's why we have both Woody Allen and Don Rickles as great American success stories. In time, it'll seem as natural to you as flatulence after consuming too much protein.

I'll never forget the time when I spent almost thirty minutes frantically looking for my sunglasses. After deciding that I had to leave the house in order to make my flight, I was bummed that I would not be able to take them with me. It wasn't until the metal detector at the airport caused the TSA attendant to tell me to place my sunglasses in a tray and put them on the belt that I noticed they were on the top of my head the entire time.

Similar situations in your life can truly be your time to let the ridiculous shine through. While it may feel strange at first, once you get the hang of it, you find that laughing at yourself (and your alone time) can be your favorite time. Once you can reliably laugh alone, laughing with others becomes much easier; especially when the accomplices come to your door so willingly.

C. Telemarketer and Solicitor Fun

They come to your home without your permission, begging for your time and your indulgence. Whether it occurs over the phone or at your door, these solicitors have given you an entirely new way to enjoy yourself. After all, they did come to you, did they not? Who are you to deny them generous portions of your wit and charm?

As kids we all played Ding-Dong-Ditch, sprinting from the mean guy's porch halfway down the block and turning the corner just as he was opening the front door wearing a scowl and his favorite flannel shirt/suspender duo, even though it was 90 degrees in the shade on that hot August afternoon. Only this is a role reversal. These are the ultimate in pranks because you're turning the intrusion around on them, and making sure you come out on top in the end. If done well (and this will come with practice), the solicitors won't know what hit them. The element of the unexpected gives you the upper hand every time.

The best way to send the door knocker (or phone solicitor) packing when they intrude unannounced and unwanted often involves a bit of acting. So, throw down your guard and have some fun, whether a newcomer to this version of uninhibited fun or a seasoned old pro. Perhaps most fun of all is that these situations always play themselves out differently, depending on the reaction of the stranger who's trying to make you their trusted friend and client.

- Tell them they're just in time to hear your Amway pitch. If they come in, have some brochures ready to start going through the plan with them; this is really good if you are a home-based business owner and can really sign them up.
- Pretend you can't see or hear them when you answer the door; look for whomever might have rung your doorbell.
- Say, "Oh, hold on a second," close the door, and don't go back no matter how often they ring the doorbell or knock.
- Heave a giant sigh and say, "You're 10 minutes too late, I'm afraid. I've already bought a Kirby."
- Greet them with a giant hug and a pat on the back.
- Play a tape of a really angry dog barking and call to them through the door to see what they want; watch them run from the house looking over their shoulder the whole way.
- If they start out by asking how you are today, answer with, "Oh, well, to be perfectly honest, this has been one heck of a day. The car didn't start, the cat got run over, my son has malaria, and I think this rash on my back is contagious."

Intruders they may be, but I don't advocate doing anything too awful to them. These are folks with a tough job trying to earn a living, often at times of the day when we're all hoping to decompress and enjoy our family (or at least a decent meal). Who among us as children sat on Santa's lap and begged for briefcases and ballpoints, proudly proclaiming we wanted to be salesmen when we grew up? The object is to have a little fun at their expense without going completely overboard. So as much as you may want to greet them with a bucket of ice water, remember they're just people trying to do a job. Save the water for the next time your buddy comes over to borrow a wrench.

On the phone you have more leeway, both in what you can say and how comfortable you'll be saying it. Since they can't see you, the odds that you'll be more willing to play with them increase dramatically. In fact, as our pre-teen days have proven, phone fun can rarely be beat.

- Answer the phone with a ransom demand.
- Answer saying. "City Morgue."
- Order a pizza from them; insist on no anchovies.
- Let them talk without interruption until they realize you haven't responded; when they say, "Hello?" pretend to have just gotten on the phone and ask them to repeat what they just said; do this repeatedly until they hang up.
- Act hard of hearing.
- Pretend their spiel is the secret code to a military operation.

- While speaking to them, randomly insert bits from various songs.
- Ask the caller to marry you; it's even funnier if they're the same gender.
- Insist that the caller is a friend playing a joke on you; reply with, "Oh knock it off, Jim! I know it's you. How's your wife? The kids doing well?"
- Start asking them a bunch of questions like how to spell their name, how to spell the company name, then start getting more personal. Ask them how long they've worked where they are, do they like it, would they consider getting your daughter a job there, if it's a long commute for them, keep going until they hang up on you.

- Just keep saying, "Sure!" over and over again, even while they're talking until they figure out that you're not serious.
- Tell them to talk real slow, because you like to write every word down!
- Ask them if they're close by because you've fallen out of your wheelchair and need help getting up.

One of my favorite things to do is whenever a solicitor calls and starts their pitch, I ask them to talk really slow because I like to write every word down. If you ham this up and ask for the spelling of extremely easy words as they are talking, you will find that they are quick to end your call. Everyone has their own way of handling unwanted solicitors. Take notes and keep them handy. It's a lot more fun than just saying, "No thanks; not interested," I assure you, and it may even convince a few people to take the solicitor block off their phones.

D. Exciting Pet Plans

Your pets are the most forgiving creatures you'll ever meet and will provide hours of entertainment if you ask them, and yet, for some reason these valuable assets are often overlooked. They live to please you and if that means inadvertently joining in on your fun, so be it. They only ask for a little attention in return for playing along.

Most of these involve a little forethought and set-up, but the laughter factor can't be beat.

- Here is one for the ladies, or a really comfortable man: Buy matching tutus for you and your pet; wear them on your evening walks.
- Take your cat out for a stroll on a leash.
- Tie a string around your waist letting one end dangle to the floor for your kitty to play with while you go about your chores.
- Give your dog a Mohawk.
- Play jungle noises to see how your pets react.
- Spray paint your pet with washable hair dye in fluorescent colors before taking him shopping at the local pet store.

- Drag a collar attached to a leash around the neighborhood as if you were walking a dog; call to him often and say, "Good dog!" whenever you tell him to stay or sit.
- Teach your dog to howl whenever you sing; break out into song randomly.
- Attach a sock to a fishing line and "fish" for a cat.
- Get a laser pointer and have the cat try to catch it. This is my favorite thing to do with my cat, Mickey.

Remember that these wonderful creatures have no shame. Embarrassment is entirely a human trait, and this should be considered whenever possible. Ignore the nay-sayers who get embarrassed for your pooch's new 'do'. Like Kill-joy, they're thinking of their own discomfort; not that of the dog. The most discomfort your pet will have is taking the bath to get rid of the color.

In the end, the objective is to believe that your home is your place to find comfort and pleasure in all you do. It's also the best place to practice finding fun in the everyday things. Take the time to keep it funny here and you'll notice big changes in the rest of your life.

Chapter 4

Keep It Funny On The Road

My profession keeps me on the road a lot. I've traveled through nearly all 50 states performing at various functions while doing over two hundred shows a year. I know what it's like to be tired and cranky driving from point A to point B with dimwit navigators all around, but I work really hard at not letting it bother me. There are far too many real problems out there to let a little aggressive driving get me down. Real problems exist on the road that should command our attention, like finding the next rest stop after drinking 48 ounces of coffee or knowing which exit offers a selection of nutritious, vegetarian meals. Besides, there are already enough people in the world taking the whole "road rage" thing too seriously.

The statistics on road rage are scary. According to the only real study done to date on the effects of aggressive driving, The recent Mizell Report commissioned by AAA, there were over 10,000 accidents from January 1, 1990 to August 31, 1996 attributed to aggressive driving resulting in 218 deaths of men, women, and children with another 12,610 injuries. With a compound growth rate of 7%, that indicates the problems are only going to get worse. That means there were on average around 1,480 accidents a year caused by road rage. And that was ten years ago! With the 7% increase, we're looking at something like 2100 per year now. What is going on out there?!

It's time to stop the madness and get back to enjoying ourselves whenever and wherever we can; which most definitely includes the car. When driving becomes an unpleasant task, it's time to find ways to make it a fun excursion, and possibly make some friends – instead of enemies – as you go.

A. Don't Get Mad; Get Friendly!

Don't let the actions of a few overly aggressive people affect your attitude for the day. You have a choice. You can either flip out and flip off the idiot behind you for driving too closely or you can slow down, smile a big grin in the mirror while waving fanatically as if to a long, lost friend. Which one makes for a better day all the way around? After all, when you take control of the situation and make it one filled with laughter, you're replacing a whole lot of unhealthy anger with life-saving humor and maybe doing the same for the other driver.

Nothing, I repeat *nothing* is so important that it's worth risking life and limb. Don't endanger yourself to get back at someone else or to prove a point. Tailgating will not decrease your blood pressure or assist in relaxing the other passengers in your car. Instead, take the path of least resistance and play with them or find ways to make them laugh along with you. So stop getting angry and instead, get friendly. At the very least, get goofy.

- Pretend to pick your nose when the kids look at you; for some of you this could already be in your arsenal by default.
- When another driver honks at you, honk back to the tune of "Shave and a Haircut".
- Honk and wave at strangers.

- Bark at dogs in other vehicles.
- Get the attention of the driver or passenger of a neighboring car and toss foam balls at them; keep your windows rolled up while you do this.
- Pretend to pick bugs out of your hair and eat them; best done when behind a school bus.
- Next time you accidentally do something wrong and someone gives you a "gesture". Do not give it back. Instead, do what I said at the beginning of the chapter and wave to them like you know who they are. Stop the hate on the roads!

The object is not to let what others do irritate you. Instead, make them opportunities to laugh while making fun at the absurdity of getting uptight during a drive. Congestion is increasing, we all know that. Commutes everywhere are getting longer. Gas prices are skyrocketing from the merely ridiculous to the obscene. There are times when all of us will be 20 minutes behind schedule for unanticipated reasons and the traffic before us will come to a complete stop. It's Murphy's Law. When (not if) you are suddenly stuck in traffic, enjoy that time and make the best of it. Stash an audio book or your favorite comedy CD in the car for these occasions. With a little luck, doing things like this might even teach other drivers a thing or two about chilling out instead of getting all heated up. Life is serious enough without adding to it by getting worked up over road courtesy, or lack thereof. Remember, the idea is to keep it funny!

B. Daily Commute

The dullest, most uninteresting part of every day is commute time. Whether the drive is fifteen minutes or an hour and fifteen minutes, that's time wasted out of your precious day… if you allow it. On the other hand, it can be a great time for freewheeling fun.

The danger here is letting other drivers get under your skin. We've discussed reports indicating that millions of Americans suffer from "rage disorder" most often erupting on the road, so taking steps to keep a happy, upbeat attitude as you manipulate through throngs of traffic will make for a much healthier outlook on life. The trick is to avoid taking it all so seriously.

I think that many of the Kill-joys of the world are simply soldiers in training for potential road rage combat. Our emotional health relies on our ability to successfully address the multiple and competing stresses of life. Often our failure to recognize the rising stress level or remove ourselves from situations that will escalate it, results in outbursts that really are misdirected. Have you found yourself asking why you screamed at the dog for not telling you there was no food left in the 20-pound bag lying on the floor of the garage? Or why you snapped at your spouse for leaving just a drop of coffee to burn at the bottom of the pot? We need to control the things we can and let go of those we can't. Driving into that unexpected bottleneck is a perfect opportunity. Make a conscious decision to not light that fuse of yours. Instead, throw yourself headfirst into the following list, not the front end of that Hummer riding your bumper, no matter how much he might deserve it.

- Sing along to the radio as dramatically as you can, especially at stoplights.
- Look suspiciously at the car next to you at a stoplight, then reach over and make sure your door is locked, never taking your eyes of the other person.
- When someone cuts you off, honk and give them a thumbs up signal with a big grin.
- Rev your engine at a red light and look at your neighbor like you want to race, and then casually move forward when the light turns green.
- Shoot silly string out your window as you drive along the road; it might be funnier if you have your windows up.
- Glue several very strong magnets to the bottom of an old mug and put it on top of your car; smile and wave back at anyone trying to get your attention.
- Put old bolts in your hubcaps for a musical drive to work and watch what others do when they hear it.
- Roll down your window and ask people if they have any Grey Poupon®.
- Whistle the first seven notes of "It's a Small World" incessantly.
- Blow you nose and offer to show the contents of you Kleenex® to other passengers.

- Bet the other passengers you can fit a quarter in your nose.

One gentleman, annoyed with the constant honking in traffic, put a sign in the back window of his car. It read: "Honk if you see this sign." It did a great job of lightening his mood because he had no idea who was honking at him and who was honking at his sign. In the end, whenever someone honked at him, he honked back, as did many of the nearby drivers. It made for a chipper, musical drive to work while eliminating the frustrating "beeps" from before.

Driving has its own unique frustrations, but it also has a series of benefits over other types of commuting. Having control over one's own time gives the solo driver some peace of mind. The radio, car temperature and comfort settings remain constant with the driver's wants and needs for a relatively peaceful drive to the office. These meditative times are useful for both getting into gear for a productive day at work, as well as for decompressing when the day is done.

Not all of us are drivers. Some of us need to rely on public transportation. While starting and ending the day being pressed against masses of other people may not do much for a positive attitude, the potential for fun is significantly higher. These are most likely the people who need fun as much – or more – than you do. Take the chance to look the fool and I bet you'll be surprised at how many people are willing to play along just because they need the respite from their own dreary existences.

Regular public transit users know there is a complex set of unwritten rules governing proper transit etiquette. These often put the traditional social handcuffs that bind our friends the Kill-joys to shame. Silence is something to be respected and honored, with the banter and brash behaviors limited to the lowest form of life (tourists) or those closest to them on the social ladder (teenagers).

- When getting on the train or bus, smile brightly and say, "Hi!" to everyone who meets your eye.
- Have a puppet show with your hands, maybe even bring a puppet and put on a show.
- Learn some magic and put on a show. (www.keepitfunnystore.com)
- Say "Happy Birthday!" to random people.
- If forced to stand, face the back of the bus or train the entire trip.
- Say, "Oh! I know this place!" at every stop.
- Read the comics or a funny book aloud; or at least laugh hysterically every few minutes.
- Complain that it's too hot regardless of what temperature in the car; after the driver adjusts the temperature, complain it's too cold.
- Bring a pocket of suckers and hand them out to everyone you meet.
- Learn to yodel and put on a show.
- Every time you go over a really big bump or stop suddenly, scream "We're gonna' die!"

- Bring a radio and suggest a game of musical chairs.
- Sit down and pull out a handful of brown lunch bags opening them and setting them up around you; turn to your neighbor and say, "I get motion sickness. Do you have any bags with you in case I run out?"
- Scream every time someone pulls the cord for a stop.
- If anyone brushes against you, jump back and scream, "Bad touch!"

Little by little the daily grind of commuting will get to everyone. Take steps to be sure it doesn't happen to you or those with whom you commute; be they friends or strangers. Before long, you'll have everyone wondering just what you'll pull next and you may find that you surprise yourself as you try to top the last bit of fun.

C. Long Trips Make for Great Times

The relatively short drives to and from work are one thing, but what do you do when driving for hours and hours across desert, mountains and plains? Why, return to your roots and play the games you did as a child, of course. I remember as a kid that every car ride was an adventure, the joy of being thrown around in the car at every stop due to not wearing your seat belt may not happen anymore, but one of the things that will work is the alphabet game. My mom would start by saying, "A-Apple," my brother would say, "A- Apple B-Banana" I would then follow with, "A-Apple B-Banana C-Cantaloupe" and then back to my mom. This would continue until someone forgot a letter and word or we made it to Z. I don't remember ever actually making it to the end, but what fun it was to try. And of course there is "I see something in this car and the color is…" This is still a winner. How about name that tune? The possibilities are endless

When the weather's nice – or even if it's not so nice – turn off the air-conditioning, roll down the window and play with the air currents against your arm. There is nothing cooler than the feeling of the hair on your arm when you bring it back in the car. Here are a few more things to try:

- Pump your arm up and down when you pass a semi truck to get them to honk.
- Run around the building every time you stop before going inside.
- Wear your pajamas and carry a teddy at rest stops.
- Make up new names for the places you pass.
- Play the alphabet game: look for words beginning with the letters of the alphabet in order on signs, passing vehicles and buildings.
- Take a random exit ramp; ask for direction to the town you're in. When they tell you you're there, look confused, glance at your map and scream "Oh no!... Wrong state…" and walk out.
- Have a prepared sports bottle with water and yellow food coloring. Squirt it under the walls of neighboring stalls, yelling "whoops. Sorry about that."
- Stop at out-of-the-way and bizarre museums along the way.
- Keep a CD or tape of kiddy songs in the car to sing along.

If you have company on the trip, there are more options available to you. Have someone read to you from one of your favorite books or make up a story with each of you saying two sentences before passing it on to the next person. With small children in the car, do a round robin of counting to see how far you can get before someone makes a mistake.

Anything is better than monotonous scenery as you barrel along, but remembering the fun things you did as a kid to pass the time will keep you in good spirits along the way. Well, just about anything. Don't do anything that might lead to a dangerous situation. Have fun, sure, but not at the expense of your safety. Seatbelts on, eyes focused, hands on the wheel and both feet on the floor. If that's all in place, then go for it.

D. Around the block in 80 ways

Walking has benefits beyond the merely physical. There was a study published in the *Annals of Behavioral Medicine* that showed university students who walked and did other moderate exercise regularly had lower stress levels than those who did nothing or even those that exercised strenuously. This is why many people walk for the mental well-being more than just to stay in shape. My wife and I try to walk a couple of times a week through our neighborhood trails. It gives us time to leave 'life' behind and enjoy the beauty of the trees and streams, share stories, vent to each other about our day/week, and most importantly, to laugh. This is a huge stress reliever. Not everyone can have a walking partner, but don't let that stop you. Walking alone has just as many benefits.

Walking can lead to the release of the body's natural happy pill – endorphins. The higher the heart rate during the walk; the more endorphins are released. It also gives you time to think, as well as time to get away from the 'day'. Just getting out of a stressful environment, breathing in some fresh air and feeling your body move will release stress. If you still need more reasons to get out and walk, here are a few more:

- It will put not only a physical, but mental distance between you and your stressful environment.
- It gives you time to clear your head, and a clear mind can help you through problems and possibly find solutions as you are walking.
- It will give you a chance to reconnect with yourself.
- It will make you feel better about yourself for investing in good health.

The American population, as a whole, is much more sedentary than ever before. Languishing in front of the television or computer has surpassed baseball as the national pastime. Why? Because exercise for the purpose of exercise isn't very interesting, and as such, a trip to the grocery store a few blocks away is often done by car rather than foot.

The idea of taking a stroll for *fun* is completely lost on most. Therefore, in the interest of being a healthier and less stressed nation, it is time that the simple pleasure of walking is reinstated... with a twist, of course. Despite the visage of Kill-joy sitting on a neighboring front porch, taking a turn around the block can be a heck of a good time.

- Skip around the block backwards.
- Challenge anyone you meet to a jump rope contest.
- Play Chicken with anyone else on the sidewalk.
- Don't step on a crack; jump over them instead.
- Flip a coin to decide which way to go: heads means right, tails means left, off the sidewalk means straight.
- Dance your way down the street; music is optional.
- Pretend to be a pirate; close one eye and say, "Argh!" to those you meet.

Shove Kill-joy into the closet before you take off for parts unknown and relax on the way. Walks can be made even more fun when you include the kids. They often have their own style of fun that makes these seem almost amateurish. Follow along and learn as best you can; it's your best bet to a long, healthy life.

Chapter 5

Keep It Funny On The Job

For most, no less than 40 hours each week are spent on the job. A person's attitude most often means the difference between a promotion and stagnation. How can you keep your attitude positive and your mind fresh? Focus on being a proactive, team player in order to develop the needed synergies and level the playing field for you, your boss, and the customers your organization serves? Laughter, of course, is the right answer, but you need to do it with class. Know when your humor will be most appreciated and how to apply it to the best audience.

The atmosphere in today's business world is open and inviting fun while maintaining strong guidelines on productivity. Largely gone from the halls of most employers are the starched shirt, suit and formal wear of the past. Open collars and even open toes are much more common than ever before. Use this level of informality to your advantage as you go through your day and you'll find that you enjoy being at work more than ever before. There are limits, and of course a time and a place for everything. Consult your employee handbook if there's any question whether a line you're considering as optional to cross is really a form of insubordination or unwelcome harassment. Better yet, schedule an appointment with your human resources director. Bring a copy of the manual in Braille and admit there are parts you don't quite understand and would appreciate some guidance in interpreting.

Unlike a lot of performers today, I prefer to keep my material fun for the whole family. I strive on going to the edge, but never going over. I enjoy pushing people's limits of laughter. Having a good time doesn't have to mean being vulgar, and in fact, I like to think that it's a sign of real talent to be able to avoid the easy shots. This is how I spend my time, and I want to be comfortable doing it no matter where I happen to be. Whether I'm at a comedy club, on a University campus, in Las Vegas or at a company event, I tailor my act for my audience, but it's still a show that anyone can see and appreciate. This is important to note, because when you go out there on your own and start pushing your own limits, you're going to have to know where to stop before crossing the line.

A. Appropriate vs. Inappropriate Office Fun

The office is probably not the best place to push the limits unless you work in a very forgiving environment, like the circus. There are levels of protocol that have to be followed for the sake of productivity and standards of conduct. Pulling the chair out from under your CEO at the start of a meeting probably isn't going to endear you, however hysterical it may be to us, but telling that same CEO a joke during a break just might.

This is a joke to share at the office, especially if you work with a bunch of computer programmers: *A man was crossing the road one day when a frog called out to him and said, "If you kiss me, I'll turn into a beautiful princess." He bent over, picked up the frog, and put it in his pocket. The frog spoke up again and said, "If you kiss me and turn me back into a beautiful princess, I will tell everyone how smart and brave you are and how you are my hero." The man took the frog out of his pocket, smiled at it, and returned it to his pocket. The frog spoke up again and said, "If you kiss me and turn me back into a beautiful princess, I will be your loving companion for an entire week." The man took the frog out of his pocket, smiled at it, and returned it to his pocket. The frog then cried out, "If you kiss me and turn me back into a princess, I'll stay with you for a year and do ANYTHING you want." Again the man took the frog out, smiled at it, and put it back into his pocket. Finally, the frog asked, "What is the matter? I've told you I'm a beautiful princess and that I'll stay with you for a year and do anything you want. Why won't you kiss me?" The man said, "Look, I'm a computer programmer. I don't have time for a girlfriend, but a talking frog is cool."*

Feel free to insert your own position in the punch line to give it a touch of your personality, but remember to be conscious of with whom you're talking. The point is to be witty without being offensive.

Here's another one that cracks me up: *A pig and a hen were walking down the country road and saw a sign in a restaurant window: Ham and Eggs $4.99. The hen said to the pig, "you know, we walk by this sign every day and I think to myself, I feed these people day in and day out, I'm so proud." The pig said to the hen, "for you it may be pride but for me it's a total commitment."*

Learn how to gauge your audience's reaction by watching when they laugh. Keeping your antics within range of that will keep you on the right side of the boss. If you recognize that this isn't one of your strongest suits, limit your shenanigans to break times and coworkers rather than those higher up the salary chain. The general attitude in your office will guide you on what you can and should do, and which offices really enjoy having a good time poking gentle fun at their co-workers.

I recall reading a real life example where after laser eye surgery the patient's officemate took it upon herself to make large, glaring signs with arrows for everything in the office to help out her buddy. She made signs that read **DOOR, KEYHOLE – INSERT KEY HERE, CHAIR, DESK, COMPUTER, KEYBOARD**, etc. Though her officemate was in a bit of pain and slightly embarrassed by the big dark glasses he was forced to wear, the mood lightened considerably when he saw the signs all around. In fact, he left several up for months afterwards because they made him chuckle. It was a "feel good moment" that made everyone in the department giggle a bit. This is the emotion you should shoot for when considering whether your prank is appropriate in your particular office. Mean-spirited play doesn't work around the water cooler and should be avoided at all costs.

Nonetheless, even the stuffiest lawyers' offices need to let loose every now and then and why not be the one to relax things? Having a reputation for bringing everyone back to center during stressful times can only benefit your career – as well as your mental health – while on the job. Some companies live in a perpetual state of stress and confusion by their very nature. For instance, my wife works with children diagnosed with emotional and behavioral disorders; which is about as stressful as you can get. As much as she loves her job, it can be pretty tough on her. Many people in those kinds of situations don't last long in their chosen field because of how difficult it is to endure each day. Laughter can be the foremost preventative element for burnout in these types of careers.

There are some standard rules when it comes to office fun that must be followed from a purely common sense standpoint:

- Vulgar or pornographic images have no place in the office, nor do sexual innuendoes or jokes.
- Avoid gags and activities that make fun of religion, as well. There's no need to alienate your coworkers or supervisors by accidentally stepping on their religious convictions; these tend to be areas where even those with the best sense of humor fails.
- Politics can be fair game if the climate in your office is ripe for it, but know just how far you can push. It's better to err on the side of caution than to spend the next day cleaning out your desk.
- If you harbor ill will toward someone, then do not engage in pranks involving them (your sense of fairness may not be all that surefooted).

- Don't mess with someone's food; allergies are far too common (as are digestive illnesses like diabetes) to play around here.

The age-old advice of not discussing money, politics, religion or sex in mixed company fares well in this platform. If Kill-joy would faint at the topic, leave it alone. The good news is that his stuffiness is good for something. Leave off the more questionable antics for your college buddies or for off-the-clock hours.

B. Downtime is your most productive humor time

Even the most efficient and industrious companies have their down times, and these are the best times to find humor on the job. Since a lot of downtimes come after some very harrowing problems, these are the best times to horse around a little and regenerate the humor factor around you. In fact, your coworkers will likely thank you for relieving everyone's stress and it will give the office a feeling of renewal to tackle the next major project.

Some fun ways to enjoy break or lunch time:

- Bring in a giant bouquet of balloons and pass them around the office.
- Fill a common cupboard with ping pong balls.
- Use a binder clip and clip the sleeves of a jacket or sweater hanging on your victims chair, enjoy the confusion when they try to put it back on.

- Make paper airplanes and throw them over the cubicle wall; point to someone else when they come around to see who did it.
- Staggered throughout the week unplug different parts of your co-workers' computer. Start with the mouse, then the ten-key pad, then the monitor, and even the keyboard. If unplugging is not really an option, just put some scotch tape over the roller ball of the mouse and you will have some fun.
- Glue a quarter to the floor in your office, the break room, outside the front door, anywhere. Just place it where you will be able to watch people try to pick it up.
- Leave a message on someone's voice mail, please call Mr. G. Raffe. And leave the number to the local zoo.
- If there is a coat rack at work, turn all the coats, sweaters, overcoats, hats, mittens or anything else you find inside out. At the end of the day you will have some fun watching the confusion. My suggestion is to place your coat there and turn it inside out as well to make you appear innocent.
- Make up stories about your pen out loud.
- Have roller chair derbies around the office.
- Roll a large piece of paper up like a cigarette and go out for a break with the smokers; ask for a light.
- Put sticky notes all over your co-worker's desk while he or she is away.
- Walk into someone's office and turn the light on and off 10 times

while they watch you. If they ask you why, look at them like they're crazy and leave without answering.

- Rearrange a co-worker's desk so that it looks exactly the same, only in a mirror image.
- After a particularly stressful meeting or conference call, take a deep breath and then bark like a dog to clear your head.
- Havc a snowball fight during lunch.
- Get some hair extensions that match an officemate's hair color and leave clippings around their desk and chair over the course of a week or so; watch them constantly run to the washroom to check their hair.
- Make several copies of paperclips, put the copies in the feed tray, and watch as people go nuts trying to find the paperclip in the copier.
- Tape down the button on an officemate's phone so that it continues to ring even after the hand piece is picked up.
- Greet people in the elevator like Mork from Ork, saying, "Nanoo nanoo!"
- Walk like Groucho Marx around the office; fiddle with a fake cigar while you do so.

Playing games in the office is great fun, but there are dozens of ways to create a cohesive team mentality outside the stuffy confines of the building, and even outside of work hours.

One of the worst parts about growing up and getting a job is the loss of team fun we had in school. When was the last time you played in a league of any sort? Have you spent any time cheering for your friends on the field since high school? Now that was fun! Well, you may no longer be in school, but you may find that your co-workers miss that kind of thing as much as you.

Contact your local park district to find out what types of leagues they offer in each season, and put up a few flyers around the office to see who's interested. Most park districts have at least softball, basketball and flag football, but a few may have some of the more unusual sports, like dodge ball and badminton. Think outside the box and find something that's unique for your crew to dig into. Heck, there may even be a sandcastle or snowman building competition open to teams.

Even those not interested in playing sports can get into the action by coming along to cheer. And if league action doesn't do it for you, there are lots of other options.

Start here:

- Bring in lawn darts and have a week-long tournament.
- Create a Frisbee golf course around the office using trees and light poles as targets.
- Ask the company to supply an air hockey table or buy a used one at a garage sale and ask if you can bring it in.

(GREAT stress reliever)

- Have a monthly Karaoke date at a nearby place for the whole crowd.
- Plan ahead by bringing in an extra set of clothes and have a water fight on a particularly hot day.
- Fill a piñata with fast food gift cards, candy, and coupons for casual days; then give everyone a chance at it; make it really fun and dress it up in a suit and tie.
- Bring in a charcoal grill and make hamburgers and hotdogs for the whole team for lunch; be sure to wear your favorite goofy chef's apron and hat.
- Make a Hop Scotch board out of printer paper taped together and use a paperclip for the rock; make a tournament out of it.
- Race a friend up the wrong escalator.

At the very least, you should take 10 or 15 minutes out of your day every day to laugh, no matter how you make it happen. Whether you are stuck behind a desk or pumping a jackhammer on an overpass, you can always create opportunities to laugh at work. Find a website with clean, funny jokes and read them out loud to your coworkers or bring a book of comedy shorts to browse through for a few minutes over lunch. Keeping yourself in a good mood will go a long way toward keeping everyone else that way. It's like a reciprocal gift you give yourself.

C. Keep laughing without losing productivity

There will be a group of people who believe the old myths about the workplace. Things like *"Work is no place for fun!"* or *"If you're laughing, you must be goofing of; which is wasting valuable time and resources."* I'm sorry, but if I had to spend 40 hours each week doing anything, I want it to be fun! I don't want to dread getting up each morning facing the day in front of me. Neither should you. Besides, research shows that humor makes the day go better, not worse, in terms of productivity. If you take a moment to research this topic you will find numerous studies showing that there is a direct relationship between the company profit and the happiness of the employees.

Robert Half International conducted a study to see just how much more productive people with a sense of humor are compared to their counterparts. After surveying vice presidents and personnel directors at 100 of America's largest corporations, the study showed that 84 percent believed employees who laughed were more productive. In the same study, 97 percent of executives counted humor as one of the most valuable assets in the business place. The perception of laughter on your abilities is amazing, but it's not all smoke and mirrors. A good sense of humor can do more for your career than steadily plodding through each day.

Laughter in the work place generally means higher productivity, more creative solutions and fewer absences. There's a reason that business consultants regularly discuss team building projects involving fun and games these days: the climate in the workplace is changing from the dull, drab and boring of old. Evolving dress codes are just one example. Of course, when it comes to having fun while staying productive, as we've said, there's a delicate balance that needs to be respected.

Individual morale affects the team as a whole, and the company by default. If even a single person makes an effort to change the dynamics at work, it will have a ripple effect on everyone. That positive attitude increases communication; which is the single most important aspect of any job. Let's face it; no one wants to talk to Kill-joy. Avoiding it, however, stifles communication within the team and effectively stifles productivity.

In order to improve productivity in the workplace, it requires a shift of mentality by everyone. The old-fashioned concept of negative feedback to push for higher productivity is lost in today's business world – no matter what the business. Employees know there are other places more in tune with their morale, and they have no problem moving on. Increased turnover reduces productivity while the company strives to get new employees up to speed and hopefully retain them. The end result is a revolving door of unhappy employees and a significant drop in efficiency. What a nightmare!

The key is to remain serious about your work without taking yourself too seriously. Stay focused on the job-at-hand when it requires your attention. No amount of fun will make up for a missed deadline or an irritated client because there were jokes to be told or pranks to be pulled. The desired end result is a fun work environment with strong communication that gets the job done. Keep this in mind at all times.

Luckily, there are lots of things you can do in an off-the-cuff way that neither stifles production nor offends the schedule. In fact, even a walk to the printer can be the perfect moment for entertainment during a busy time:

- Play Duck, Duck, Goose on your way to the printer or washroom.
- Babble incoherently at a co-worker and then say, "Did you get all that? I don't want to have to repeat myself."
- Every time someone turns a page during a meeting, make a beeping noise.
- Open the cap of a White Out bottle and tip the bottle over onto a piece of wax paper spilling a generous amount. Wait a day or two until it dries, and then remove the wax paper. Take it with you to work and place it on the "neat freak's" desk.
- If you ever accidentally leave your fly open and when someone points it out to you leave it and say, "Thanks, but I really prefer it this way."
- Lock all your joints and walk around like a zombie.
- Pretend your mouse is a CB Radio.

- Do aerobics at your desk while humming "YMCA".
- Blow bubbles.
- Put up "Please Use Other Door" signs on all doors going into the office.
- Wear a "Kick Me" sign on your shirt – preferably in front so that everyone knows you know it's there.
- Every time the phone rings, yell "We've got a big one!"
- Name your computer, work truck, or the piece of machinery that you work with; talk to it every day and refer to it by name when discussing it with others.
- Sign your e-mails with *"Grazie", "Domo Origato"* or *"Danke"* instead of "Thanks".
- Suggest that only those with a low IQ can't whistle.
- Never use contractions and always refer to yourself in the third person.
- Put your garbage can on your desk and label it "IN".
- Develop an unnatural fear of an object of your choice.
- Put a mosquito netting hood over your head. Play a tape of jungle sounds all day.
- Show people your driver's license and demand to know if they've seen this person.
- Stare at static on a display TV and challenge other employees whether they, too, can see the "hidden picture."

If you have to take an elevator to get to your office or cubical, try some of these.

- Offer nametags to everyone. Wear yours upside-down.
- Make race car noises when anyone gets on or off.
- When arriving at your floor, grunt and strain to yank the doors open. Then act embarrassed when they open by themselves.
- Greet everyone getting on the elevator with a warm handshake and ask them to call you Admiral.
- Crack open your briefcase or purse, and while looking inside ask: "Do you have enough air in there?"
- Ask each passenger getting on if you can push the button for them.

Productivity requires creativity, and that thrives in a fun-filled environment. So even during the busiest times, it makes sense to take time to laugh. In fact, laughter may help drive productivity beyond expectations. Take Google™ for instance. The company thrives on having fun and look at the success they have achieved. The work environment includes a slide, game room, igloos for meeting 'pods', and it even has beanbag chairs. About.com gave this one of many examples: 'All the Engineers at Google™ are encouraged to spend 20% of their work time on projects that interest them. Not only does this keep Engineers happy and challenged, it's also good business'. Some estimates directly attribute half of all new product launches to projects that came from the 20% time program.

In the end, it serves the higher purpose of any company to have a fun work environment. People are more inclined to stay at a company where they enjoy going to work each day. Atmosphere is one of the top three things potential employees look at when they apply for a position, and a sense of humor is often looked for in the interviewing process.

So while it's important to know your stuff, it seems more important to be able to do your job with a positive attitude and a sense of humor. My suggestion to every working person who agrees with that statement: You owe it to yourself and to the continued growth of your company to follow the right chain of command and work to take baby steps in this direction. How? Make at least a yearly, but much better, a monthly commitment to an organization-wide "fun day.' Watch what happens.

Chapter 6

Keep It Funny At College

As if an office weren't bad enough, the classroom is a hotbed of boredom. After an evening of revelry at the… er… library, the droning of professors about "...the average air speed velocity of a…" can make an insomniac throw out their Ambien®. The object is to make your time *outside* the classroom as fun and funny as possible so that you can fully concentrate inside the classroom. Keeping things light will also help keep the angst of the college experience at bay.

There are constructive strategies to control the stress of college work given by campus counselors and advisors worldwide. Time management tops the list when it involves a set daily schedule with time for meals, exercise, classes and studying. Stick to this schedule every day and it will relieve the burden of last-minute projects with no time for unwinding. When making up your schedule, remember to prioritize. Mix and match difficulties and most important of all, leave time for play.

There's no doubt about it, once you leave the cushion of childhood behind, life becomes progressively tougher. The stress of more difficult class work with grades that can determine your future is only one factor in the bedlam of the undergraduate world. For many, this marks the first time away from home and the responsibilities accompanying that transition. It is not an easy thing to completely start over; which is what college is all about. College students are arguably among the most 'stressed out' individuals around. You'll have nightmares about failing college for the rest of your life. You may as well enjoy the process while you're there.

As long as there have been Universities (which is well over a thousand years), the student body has participated in unrestrained fun. The tradition of University pranks goes so far back it's become legendary in many places. Perhaps "urban legends" in some cases, but hysterical, nonetheless.

I performed my comedy magic act for the University of Iowa; where I was told about two dorms, Rienow and Slater Halls. Both of them were nearly identical in structure and appearance, with their red brick and evenly placed windows squatting on the west end of campus and separated by Grand Avenue. Stories have been relayed for decades about the rivalry between these two dorms and the antics that rivalry produced. Rumors abound about engineering students building complex catapults on the roof of one to blast various items across to the other. Tales of water balloons, buckets of shaving cream, and even an old lounge chair have reportedly made their way across the street dividing them. How much of this is true and how much is legend? I'm not sure anyone knows anymore, or cares. My guess is that as long as those tales are told, there will be someone willing to try them out for themselves.

The Yale-Harvard rivalry is hardly new, dating back over one hundred twenty years. On November 20, 2004, however, it was taken to a new high – or low – depending on which side you were on. That day, the Elis (Yale students and alumni) were facing the Cantab (Harvard students and alumni) crowd for the 121st Yale-Harvard football game. The Harvard Pep Squad (a group of 20 Elis dressed in custom-made t-shirts and wearing red war paint) jumped, preened, screamed and cheered for the Harvard team for one and a half quarters. They tossed t-shirts to the crowd and passed out sheets of red and white construction paper to spell out a rousing cheer for the 1800 Harvard fans. Halfway through the second quarter, the crowd was called upon to show their spirit by raising the construction paper high above their heads, expecting to see, "Go Harvard!" Instead, the Yale side was treated to a golden moment as the Harvard fans spelled out, "We suck!" in glorious Harvard red and white Technicolor.

This was a spin-off of a prank performed during the 1961 Rose Bowl when Cal-Tech, miffed at being left entirely out of the festivities even though it was held in their own backyard, hacked into the computer animated scoreboard and replaced the University of Washington and Illinois scores with Cal-Tech and MIT. Cal-Tech was comfortably in the lead, of course. For an added bonus, they included a beaver, the school's mascot, scampering across the bottom of the screen. This received extraordinary attention, of course, as it was broadcast nationwide. The sad thing is that the students responsible were found and punished, even though it made for the most exciting moment of a rather dull game.

According to Neil Steinberg, author of *If at All Possible, Involve a Cow: The Book of College Pranks*, a really good college prank isn't just about making someone laugh – though that's practically required. To Steinberg, the truly great pranks leave one with a "visceral satisfaction and a kind of awe that does not fade with time nor diminish with retelling. In the narrow world of university life, so routine, so programmed and often — like life in the real world — too dull to tolerate, a prank shakes things up, breaks the boredom, and gives hope for a life filled with hidden, delightful possibility."

A good prank should not, however, harm anyone. Annoyance is one thing, but hurting someone, either physically or emotionally, crosses the line. Don't!

A. Greek goodness – fraternity pranks without the pin

One doesn't have to go overboard, however, to lighten things up. Take a page from the Greek establishment. Fraternities are known for trying to one-up each other in the mischief category. There's no need to rush in order to play their games, though. Instead, grab a bunch of buddies and try some of these:

- Ask a friend to delay your professor while you pass out a "pop quiz" in the classroom in his stead; include questions on biometric thermal energy whenever possible.
- For the guys: If your friend has a pick up truck and three of you are in the front seat, try to get the window seat. When you drive by a group of girls, tell the driver to honk while quickly ducking

down below the dash. When they look, they will see your two buddies right next to each other in the seat

- If given the chance to get into a friend's vehicle, take a bunch of paper holes from a three-hole punch and place them above the visor.
- Make a number of life-sized images of the crosswalk sign guy and put them up all over campus.
- Wearing a skin-tight, flesh colored body suit, run around campus during the lunch hour.
- Create flyer invitations to "The Best Party Ever!" with an address to a local Laundromat and slip them under the doors of your dorm mates, then do your laundry that night to see who shows up.
- Dress in a white polyester suit and head to the nearest pub for some crazy dancing.
- Make a recording of squealing tires and play it very loudly near a busy pedestrian walkway to see the reactions.
- Before walking into class, ask a classmate if they're ready for the big test. (this works best if you've got another friend willing to go along with it)
- Create official looking signs that say "Push" and "Pull" then tape them to various doors around campus – to the wrong doors, of course.
- Just FYI: If you freeze a can of shaving cream, take the cap off to watch it expand covering everything as it thaws

- If the overnight temp is below 25 degrees, get some paper towels wet and put them all over the front windshield of your friend's car. The next morning, it will be a pain in the butt to remove the icy, stuck-on paper towels (make sure they do not try to drive, even if you have to help get it off), your work will be worth the laugh.
- Before going away for the weekend leaving your roommate behind, unscrew all the light bulbs.
- Glue the caps onto several pens; offer those pens when someone asks to borrow one.
- Tape up newspaper covering the entire doorway except the top of a door that opens inward (while someone is inside); fill the space between the door and the newspaper with Styrofoam™ popcorn, then cover the rest of the opening with newspaper; when the victim opens the door, it will draw all of the popcorn into their room causing a snowing affect.

The key to these pranks is to make the biggest impact for the least amount of money in a way that won't harm anyone or your chances of graduation.

If you're looking for the acceptance of the pinned ones without the hassle of hooking up with a house, consider looking into some of the social clubs at your University or college. Haven't found anything that sounds like fun to you? Then feel free to create your own club or group with one focus – FUN. Create a catchy name for your new club and hold brainstorming sessions on ways to build events on campus. I am sure together you will collectively find better ideas, but to get you started, here are a few:

- Split your group in half; have one half – with cell phones on hand – go into the library to study, preferably in the same general area; then have the other half call their cell phones at the same predetermined time.
- Pick a day and have everyone in the group ride a complete loop on one of the campus buses in just a pair of swimming trunks or a bathing suit; make it even more fun and add flippers, goggles and snorkel.
- Rent an animal costume – preferably a dangerous animal, but a fluffy bunny could be fun, too – and have the "scary animal" chase other members of the group around campus.
- Collect stacks of pennies and walk around the main campus offering a penny for people's thoughts.

The more people you can entice into going along with these ventures, the more fun it's going to be for everyone. When you want to do a really big prank or adventure, send out an e-mail to all of your friends to see who will come join the fun. You may be surprised at just how many people are waiting for an opportunity like this to come along.

B. Dorm room drama – diffuse with dares

Putting 500 students together into one building is bound to lead to drama at some point. The trials of the classroom are minor compared to the cat fighting and caterwauling that can happen in campus housing. Aside from hundreds of personalities colliding, the anxiety of change breeds a whole new style of interpersonal relationships. Some people may even surprise themselves with how crotchcty thcy can bc.

Just because the potential for drama will be there, it doesn't mean it can't be handled with concern, care and a good dose of humor. Prevent the problems as much as you can by laughing with your floor mates as often as possible. Every little bit counts in the fight for fun, and this is a battle best fought with friends. Including them in your antics will also exponentially raise the level of hilarity as they add their own ideas and schemes to yours.

- Arm yourself and a few friends with cans of silly string and have your own game of "paint ball" in the halls of the dorm.
- Have a Battle of the Bands in the common rooms using only cans and bottles as your instruments.
- Hold a scavenger hunt for the most embarrassing items you can think of with the caveat that nothing can be store bought.
- Consider hosting an open-mike night allowing only Mother Goose rhymes for lyrics and poems.
- My good friend Mark Schnider (a.k.a. Duke), loves to do this:

Take a stance - opposite of the group you are with - on a topic such as the moon landing was a hoax or the world is truly flat – and argue it vociferously.

- Race to see who can apply a box of twenty standard band aids on their body first without overlapping them.

Building friendships should be one of your priorities in school, but sometimes finding things in common can be tricky. Not only that, but, too often people create a schedule of events and stick to it with frightening regularity. Your mission, should you choose to accept it, is to shake that up and push people out of their safety zones. Do this by creating a fun, united environment for everyone.

Imagine how much fun you could have with a "Dorm Hall Fun Night". Better yet, make it a semester-long event with each floor competing at various games once each week. For example, get a representative from two competing floors, one guy and one girl. Give them life-sized blow-up dolls and a complete set of clothing for the opposite sex (i.e. the guy dresses the doll like a girl and vice versa). The object of the game is to see who can dress their doll first. Watching this could be hilarious! A friend of mine used to perform at high schools doing a game show and one thing he did was to have four or more people racing to see who can blow up three balloons, tie them, and then sit on them until each of the balloons exploded. This must be done one balloon at a time. Good times.

How about having a molding contest with aluminum foil or clay? Have each team create a bridge made entirely from aluminum foil that has to hold a certain weight. Or have them mold various animals or objects out of clay that will then be put on display for the duration of the week. Or use both and ask them to create the creepiest alien they can.

A handful of other ideas for making "Dorm Hall Fun Night" a success:

- Host a beach ball volleyball.
- Have a hula hoop contest.
- Pit two floors against each other in a game of Walleyball – volleyball played inside a racquetball court where the ceiling and walls are fair game.
- Create a dorm tournament for Slap Jack, War or Go Fish.
- See who can catch the most fireflies (if you live where there are fireflies) in one night collecting them in a glass jar.
- Compete to see who can wrap a friend up in toilet paper – head and face included – and lead them through campus to a favorite haunt first.

These are times to create memories while building lifelong friendships. The more outlandish your behavior, the better you'll remember the times and the people with whom you shared them. The advantage of moving outside one's comfort zone in college is that it sets one up for a lifetime of merrymaking and fun. After all, they say that habits formed at Universities last forever.

C. Finals week – relieving stress the funny way

Facts, figures, phrases, theories – the last few weeks of any semester contain a plethora of information meant to be regurgitated in the most significant way possible. It's a dreadful collection of books, notes, outlines and crammed study cubicles throughout the entire campus. On some level you may very well wonder how you're expected to remember where to be and when, much less the information needed for the class. These are the things your future nightmares are made of, and any relief is likely to be welcomed with teary eyes.

The stress endured during finals week can cause some pretty severe symptoms from headaches and insomnia to anxiety attacks. There are tools to combat the stress, of course, and they should be utilized. Pay attention to your body's cues and rest when you feel tired. Despite the 48-hour cram-a-thon record your roommate claims, it doesn't do any good to pull all-nighters. It just slows you down mentally, making test taking that much more difficult. Stay away from caffeine and alcohol, too. They push the body out of whack physically; which adds even more stress to your day. Given the body's response to tension, the last thing you want to do is create more problems. Remember, the more pressure you're under, the harder it is to concentrate and be productive. Relieve the symptoms of stress however you can.

The pressure of doing well on your finals does more to hurt your concentration than two hours of sleep after a bender. With your shoulders brushing your earlobes and back so tense you're convinced someone coated it with Superglue while you slept, something has to give, and soon. Remember our earlier lessons: laughter helps wake up your brain and helps you improve focus. Time for a little break from the books:

- When the library is at its quietest, stand up and shout, "I can't take it anymore! I need noise!" and then sit down as if nothing happened, assuming the librarians will let you.
- Have a water fight for a study break.
- Race to the closest park and swing as high as you can for five minutes; then run back to your books.
- Yawn as loud and as obnoxiously as you can while stretching.
- Decorate your face with highlighters.
- Bring a pillow to a class final you're not registered for; sleep (or pretend to) until the last 15 minutes, then write down a bunch of gibberish and turn your "test" in early talking about how easy it was.

The major problem with finals week is spending so much time sedentary and studying. It curls up the body and keeps the muscles taut. Take time out of your studies to jump around, run in place or do cartwheels. Anything to get the blood flowing. Go one better and do cartwheels down the dorm hall. You might just find a few friends willing to compete against you for the most number of sequential rotations.

You've got at least four years on your own without the responsibilities of a career and house. Take advantage of this time to really live it up. Push yourself beyond your comfort zone and see how far you'll go. You may just surprise yourself, especially if you've got a good group of friends to join you. This is where one of my keep it funnies came from. A few buddies accompanied me as we went door to door in St. Cloud, Minnesota. We would tell the homeowner that we were doing a study at school regarding the effects of door-to-door sales people on the temperament of everyday homeowners. We would explain after hearing how bothered people were by 'other' door knockers that we were also selling 'no soliciting' signs for their window. You would not believe how many people actually bought the little sign, not even realizing that it was a joke.

Who knows? You may just end up on the "Top 10 Best College Pranks" list. Give it a shot, anyway.

Chapter 7

Keep It Funny On A Date

A first date may be the most stressful time in your life outside of being born or robbed. Since we've already decided that stress is a negative in the whole relationship realm (see Chapter One), your best bet for an enjoyable time is to find humor in the situation. This is also a good time to push the envelope to find out just how much of an easy going and fun loving date you're with.

Things are a little easier if you know your date ahead of time, but if you're going out with someone you don't know very well, you could be in for a very stressful night. Maybe you've been set up by a friend, you just met the person briefly before exchanging numbers or your name is Kevin and you met them on My Space. Regardless of where it started, you're now going to be with that person for a few hours to figure out where things are going. It's tough to know the best way to approach the situation and even harder to know if you're doing things "right". Relax. You're tapping into Kill-joy's attitude again, and it's going to end ugly if you do that.

Instead of worrying about where to put your hands during the movie, have fun with the moments. Take your partner somewhere unique or make the everyday date something exotic. A smile is, after all, your most attractive accessory. And remember to laugh freely. Your sense of humor will get you through this.

A. Shared Laughter: Priority No. 1

It's been said that a relationship without laughter is doomed to failure and given the statistics regarding divorce in the United States, it seems that not many people are finding humor in their homes. This being the case, finding a partner to share laughs should be the number one priority of singles everywhere.

Dr. Robert Provine, PhD, a neuroscientist, did a recent study on the benefits of laughter in relationships and found that humor and laughter are the glue that holds relationships together. “Laughter is not primarily about humor,” says Dr. Provine, “but about social relationships.”

Through laughter, people find a positive vibe that draws them closer together. Taking pleasure in a person’s company stems from the entertaining way in which they interact with you, and humor and wit are a large component of that.

The results of Dr. Provine’s study did show some interesting trends. For instance, women laugh on average 126% more than men, with men being the primary laugh-getters. This works out nicely as men tend to have a greater attraction to women who laugh heartily at their wit. Women, on the other hand, are the barometer of the connection; the more often she laughs, the happier she is in her relationship.

This is important to know before heading out into the dating world. No matter how well you dress or how polite your manners, your ability to laugh and go-with-the-flow regardless of the situation will be the deciding factor for the level of attraction. So relax and enjoy yourself. Find humor in whatever you do, and don't be afraid to laugh long and hard if the situation warrants it. No really. It's a good thing.

If you are saying to yourself that not every situation can be funny let me tell you about one of my 'first dates'. It was late October. I know this because I met this nice young lady briefly during homecoming at Saint Cloud State University and we agreed to go for dinner at a local Italian restaurant called *Ciatti's*. We did just that and the date was off to a fantastic start. At this point in the story we have to rewind about 15 years, to a water skiing accident I had as a young kid. I knocked out my front top right tooth and had to have a crown implanted. To the naked eye, you'd never guess it was anything but real.

So at that nice Italian resaurant, on that first date, I bit into a nice breadstick. As I did, the glue, epoxy or whatever weak adhesive they used to hold my crown in place decided, after many successful years, that this would be the moment it did not want to remain attached any longer and my crown thought the soft bread was a great place to lay. Now I'm not sure if you know what is beneath a crown, but just in case you need a picture it's a little peg, a small miniature tooth that alone, without the cover of a crown, looks most ridiculous. So, there I am. It's me and Mini Me staring at my date. All I could do was laugh at the situation. Now even though this date did not turn into 'true love,' even with the mishap we had a great time and it was in large part because we were able to laugh at the incident. Even the most embarrassing situation, because of laughter, can turn out to be a fun night.

B. Know your audience

As in all things to do with humor, knowing your audience is necessary to know just how far you can go. On a date, especially a *first* date, this is about as essential as you can get. There's no need to scare the person off before getting to know them. Gauge their level of shyness by how they reacted to asking or being asked out, and cater to their comfort level; at least at first.

Nonetheless, after finally getting Kill-joy off our shoulders, the last thing we want to do is saddle ourselves with a critic. Plan your dates in a way that expands both your comfort zones while still keeping things under control. This tactic will allow you both to see how you handle a challenge without making either of you feel miserable at the prospect.

As time goes on, you can let loose a bit more and see how well your date handles it. Eventually, you'll find one who can accept your nature easily, laughing at your antics rather than hiding from them; maybe even playing along with you.

From the "Take It Slow" book of options, give these a try for your next date:

- Go to a t-ball game and cheer for the home team.
- Insist on calling the server Garcon. (pronounce it gar-kon)
- Say, "Not it!" when the server asks if you're ready to order.
- Take your date to the circus instead of a movie. Besides what's the point of going someplace and not talking for two hours?
- After a picnic in the park, play a game of Leap Frog.
- Rent canoes and take a long, leisurely trip down river.
- Go to a water park and pretend to drown in the kiddy pool; get into a splash fight.
- Spend the day at an amusement park; be sure not to give the kiddy rides a pass.
- Ask if they serve paella at an Italian restaurant or tacos at a French restaurant.
- Place your Starbuck's order in Italian: *"Un doppio caffè, per favore."*

None of these will overtly distress your date and can lend a bit of frivolity at a potentially awkward time. The more relaxed the two of you are, the more likely you'll both have fun; whether there's a spark between you or not. Because really, isn't that what dating should be about?

C. Having Fun: Priority No. 2

The average person will date 100 people before finding The One™. Okay, I made up those statistics, but the truth is that finding a mate is a very hit-or-miss endeavor. Finding someone that fits all of the criteria of mate potential is hard work and rarely happens on the first try. Whatever the statistics on childhood sweethearts, one can guess they're pretty low. (That being said; I did marry my high-school sweetheart.)

This makes dating a necessary evil to just about every single person in the free world. Wow, what a way to look at it! And yet that's how many people *do* look at it. Dating is a means to an end with no real positive benefit in and of itself. It's the most ridiculous thing in the world! How often does one have the opportunity to stretch their limits with a stranger who is equally as interested in getting to know you as you are them? Well, as often as you have a date, actually, if you do things right.

Hanging out with your friends is one thing, but taking time out of your busy schedule with the hope of making at least a new friend and potentially a new partner should be treated reverently. Did I say reverently? I meant irreverently. Stop making it a serious event that requires serious thought and ambition. It's meant to be a good time, so do your best to keep it funny.

Give the following things a shot on your next date and see how they go:

- Go rock climbing.
- Test your ice skating skills together.
- Attend a Renaissance Faire in full costume.
- Visit a haunted house.
- Ballroom dance.
- Go to an improv comedy show and volunteer during audience participation.
- Make reservations at the local culinary school for dinner.
- Take a wine tasting class together.
- Play in a ball pit.

Dating should be about going out and having fun with a potential new buddy and if a connection beyond friendship is made, it's a bonus. Going to an event having expectations just leads to unnecessary stress for you both. Instead, go with an open mind about both the experience and the person and see where it leads. When all is said and done, you'll have a nice memory to treasure even if you don't have Ms. or Mr. Right to show off to the family.

D. Take it in stride – laugh at humiliation

Sometimes, despite our best intentions, a date goes terribly wrong.

Open zippers, accidental tumbles, teeth coming out and even full-blown medical emergencies can take a date from fun and flirty into the Twilight Zone. The automatic reaction for most people is to apologize profusely for the gaffe, kick themselves hard, and pray the evening will end as quickly as possible. Fortunately, if you've been paying attention, you know just what to do. You are no longer "most people" and it shows.

You've shed the shackles of Killjoy and learned that laughing at oneself is the best cure for those awkward moments. Even better, you've learned to turn those "Oh my gosh!" moments into side-splitting, knee-slapping memories to pull out on rainy days. Besides, who wants to share a boring, dull first date story with the grandkids? You may as well make yours a memorable one, even if it shakes your self-respect a bit.

Regardless of what happens while you're out, you can turn it into a gut buster if you have the right frame of mind going into the date. Nothing you do will be so important that a faux pas will destroy all of mankind. Ride it out and laugh as you go. Consider it a litmus test for your date's sense of humor and adventure, the two most important attributes.

Having said that, I'm not suggesting you go out of your way to make a complete fool of yourself. Certain rules of decency should apply regardless of how much fun you want to have. Don't over indulge.

One drink might help to loosen you up, but more than that is probably too many. In fact, on a first date, it may be smart to stay away from anything that might challenge your competency in any way. Why tempt fate, after all?

Do, however, go along with things you've never done. Can't dance? Don't worry about it! Go have fun. You've never rowed a boat? No biggie! A canoe trip down a slow moving river can be a blast if your date is willing to try it out. Afraid of heights? Maybe it's time you rode a Ferris wheel and faced that fear head-on. Never mind, that doesn't sound like a lot of fun and defeats the purpose of these outings, unless of course your purpose was to take a can of potato soup with you and dump it out when you are at the top while making vomit sounds. Okay, bad idea. Just make sure you enjoy yourself as much as you can no matter what you're doing. If you're having fun, it doesn't really matter how good or bad you are at something. And if your date has a problem with the way things are going, then maybe this isn't the right person for you, anyway.

Treat your date with respect and play along with the fun and you'll have a good time regardless. Don't try to muddle things with looking for more than a little excitement outside your normal routine.

Chapter 8

Keep It Funny During Special Occasions

Pomp and circumstance; my foot! Take advantage of the moment, but be conscious of whose day it is. There's nothing funny about stealing the spotlight from someone who's worked hard for their placc in it.

This doesn't mean they have to have all the fun, though. Special occasions are a fact of life in any community, and most of the time they can be darned tedious, even for the guest of honor. If you pick up the slack and inject a little pleasure into the party, you'll be remembered – and revered – for all times.

Just about the only special event that doesn't benefit from a little humor is a funeral; unless the guest of honor – so to speak – would have appreciated it. That's just one of those things that really should be respected because the results could be pretty awful. Anything else, though, is fair game.

A. Bring life to the event without ruining the moment

I've repeatedly gone over the concept of appropriate vs. inappropriate laughter and joking around, which is a good thing because it shows up here as well. A good number of these special events have a moment of seriousness that should be respected at all costs.

Graduations, weddings, etc., include a time of appraisal for what is occurring and the upcoming changes, and to infringe on that is just plain rude. The moment for fun comes after the pontifications, not during, so save your wit for the party after.

The urge to pull a prank, however, may be very difficult to squelch, especially during moments of intense seriousness. Should this be a problem, here are a few suggestions that might save your peace of mind:

- Bring along a large latex balloon to a graduation and let it fly free during the commencement speech.
- Write “Help” on the bottom of the groom’s left shoe and “me” on the bottom of the right; when he kneels during the ceremony, the sanctuary will see his cry for help.
- Mix up the numbers on the hymnal board.
- Get your friends involved and write a message to the audience during graduation by putting signs on the top of your caps, something like “Watch out world, here we come!”
- If giving a gift, give a puzzle with a few pieces from a similar puzzle.

Okay, there are times for a little fun during the more serious moments, which can lighten the mood. Just be careful to limit your antics to those who won’t unduly disrupt the ceremony or cause discomfort for the guest of honor. It also helps if it can’t be traced back to you. Just in case. Also, remember to do it for fun, not the attention.

B. Party? Let's Play!

Once the big to-do is over, it's time to party and this is where you get to shine. Roll up those sleeves and get down to the serious job of making laughter. From the cocktail hour to the midnight waltz, the audience is at your disposal.

Remember those magic tricks I talked about in Chapter One? Now is the time to pull out the simple card tricks for between-course fun. By now you've probably started keeping an arsenal of goodies in the trunk of your car for just such occasions. Pull out the deck of cards you've got stashed and entertain the crowd with your amazing feats of mental prowess.

Once dinner is over and the music starts, it's time to try a few of these:

- Insist that the DJ play "Gloria" and sing it to the bride
- Dance like John Travolta in *Saturday Night Fever* to every song
- Convince your table to serenade the guest of honor with Jolly Good Fellow.
- Start a Congo line during a slow song.
- If you are at tables, get your table to laugh together extremely loud every few minutes, watch as everyone in the room wants to sit at your table.

The momentum stays with you during a party. People are there to have a good time, but they don't always know the best way, especially if Kill-joy is sitting at their table. Take the initiative to move things along and those potential wallflowers will thank you, as will the guest of honor.

If you do find the handful of people who are not sure how to join the fun, single them out as your assistants in your endeavor to get the ball rolling. Showing them a little attention sometimes lifts their self-esteem just enough to get them in charge of their own fun.

C. Kids get it – and need it – the most

I always look forward to having a child or two at my table. They make the best audience and usually need the distraction more than adults. Playing with them is a special treat, but not one always appreciated.

Perhaps you haven't noticed, but when it comes to these most auspicious events, children are usually bored to tears or left off the invitation list altogether to avoid unwanted fussing. This is really a pity because when it comes to getting silly, no one gets it like children. Yes, they may squirm and fuss during the important parts, but in the end, these very same children can be the life of the party. They dance to every song, follow every cue and laugh when there really isn't much to laugh at.

All too often our society shoves children away from the more serious part of life. It may be to protect the children from boredom, but one can't help but wonder if it's not really to "protect" adults from silliness. Yuck! These excruciatingly dull events could use the giggles of children, in those moments we might need them the most.

Should you be lucky enough to be present at an event with children, make use of their ability to have fun at any moment.

- Play peek-a-boo during the more boring parts of the events.
- Start a Congo line with the youngest child you can find leading the way.
- Play Hot Potato with a real hot potato.
- Play Simon Says in the food line; whatever makes it on the plate has to be tried.
- Keep a hula hoop in the trunk for dance floor fun for all ages.
- Play Telephone around the table while waiting for the next course to be served; start out with something like, "Flying pigs on Sunday evening eat truffles."

Encourage their more creative sides and you'll be laughing in no time. Do keep in mind, however, that their parents may not be as tuned into the fun as you. Don't do anything that will get the little tikes in trouble, and remember that once that switch is flipped, it's rather hard to turn it back off.

If they get too riled up, have them play a few rounds of Graveyard to slow down. Pick one child to play the grave digger while the rest all lay on the floor pretending to be dead. The grave digger then moves around the corpses without touching them and watches for signs of life. When they pinpoint a "zombie", the grave digger calls out the zombie's name and the zombie has to help look for other signs of life. The last person dead plays the next grave digger. This is great at the end of a party to calm everyone down and the kids think it's the best game ever!

The object of this lesson is to guide kids' exuberance in a way that is fun for everyone. They're going to want to move around, play and stay active. Take advantage of this by directing it into acceptable games at the right time in a way that won't interrupt or upset the special reason you're there. There are plenty of opportunities to shake loose at just about any event if approached the right way.

Remember to focus on the host or hostess first, but don't take yourself too seriously while enjoying the festivities. Chances are the more fun you have, the more fun the guest of honor will have, too.

Chapter 9

Conclusion

Life, lemons, lemonade. You know the spiel. Instead of waiting around for sour grapes, though, take the chance to "Keep it Funny" in every aspect of your life, every day. Not only does it make your body work better, it makes life better for you and everyone around you.

I remember one Saturday afternoon; I received a notice in the mail there was a certified letter at the post office; which could be picked up on Monday. I found myself with two options I could allow myself to ponder the notion the letter contained bad news and then over the weekend my stomach would have gone into knots, my heart rate would have gone up, and I would have been as punchy as a sixth grader with ADHD. Basically, I would have been stressed out! But as my Mom used to say; "Don't borrow trouble". My second option was to consciously think that it was a sweepstakes prize and I won a million dollars. There would be no knots, no fast heart rate and I would have no need for Ritalin™. I might have even laughed about it.

It's all in your head. You control your thoughts. We all do. Life is about perception. We can take every situation and choose to think of it as the best or worst case. Any situation can either evoke anger or joy. If we could just work on assuming the best and finding the laughable side of whatever the situation, it will reduce the emotional tension; which just might be the cause of our stress. I believe that humor can and will provide an emotional distance to any issue. It can allow you to step back and evaluate the situation, letting you realize that maybe the presenting 'problem' is not that big of a deal. And in the event that it is, you will give yourself the opportunity to see there are more resources to help address – or even solve - the issue.

I realize not everything is funny and there are certainly times when laughter can be inappropriate. There are also genuine and legitimate biological brain disorders that require professional assistance to address. All I'm saying is; the next time life throws you a lemon, try to find a way to keep it funny. And remember this; every day you wake up you make the choice whether it is going to be a good or bad day! Choose wisely

Even if you look at it from a purely scientific viewpoint, our bodies were created to improve with laughter. We get healthier, stronger and happier the more we laugh and have fun. It's a stress reliever and it creates an environment of companionship. Our culture is starting to recognize this and shift toward a more relaxed way of life that just begs for creative events to make the world more interesting and fun. Even businesses are starting to get the drift and have made fun a priority. As a whole, our society is beginning to shed the stuffy, rigid requirements that Kill-joy demands. It's time to rearrange our way of thinking and do the same.

Laughter isn't something that just happens; it's a reactive choice you make every day to get you past life's obstacles. Be an active participant in your life's humor and you'll find the most amazing things will happen. You'll stand taller, your heart will be stronger, years will drop from your face and you'll have more friends than you know what to do with.

Once you put Kill-joy out of your mind, you'll find that you welcome the absurd and the ridiculous as necessary parts of your life. No matter how difficult or painful life gets, you'll find the time and desire to laugh at it. It's just life, after all, and what about that is so terribly serious it can't be laughed at? The answer is nothing.

Ignore the Kill-joys, use *your* wit to outwit the dimwits and the nitwits and have some fun. It's really simple. Try it.